The ADORNES DOMAIN and the JERUSALEM CHAPEL in Bruges

A remarkable legacy from the Middle Ages

Véronique Lambert

A
U
P

Translated from Dutch by Ian Connerty

Cover illustration: Frontcover: View of the domain from the Balstraat.
                         Backcover: Anselm Adornes. Detail of the stained
                         glass window in the Jerusalem Chapel.
Cover design: Mordicus
Lay-out: Under Cover Xpair

Amsterdam University Press English-language titles are distributed in the US
and Canada by the University of Chicago Press.

ISBN 978 94 6298 992 4
NUR 684

© V. Lambert / Amsterdam University Press B.V., Amsterdam 2018

Address: Adornesdomein, Peperstraat 3, 8000 Brugge
www.adornes.org

CONTENTS

In the following pages the reader will discover the amazing story of the Adornes family and their descendants in Bruges. This remarkable history starts around the year 1300 in Flanders and reaches a first highpoint in the 15th century with the brilliant and charismatic Anselm Adornes, who combined the qualities of a shrewd merchant, a thoughtful diplomat and a devout pilgrim in a single personality. It is to this exceptional man that we owe the most important part of the patrimony that remains visible today: the Adornes domain. This includes the patrician mansion, the garden, the almshouses and, of course, the spectacular Jerusalem Chapel.

Foreword

It is equally remarkable that the Adornes history has continued unbroken over six centuries, surviving storms and setbacks, the secularism of the French Revolution, the fury of two world wars and the inevitable periods of disinterest. In scarcely three generations, the Adornes were able to create such a strong familial and patrimonial identity that the following generations could rely on a heritage sufficiently full of responsibility and resources to allow them to ensure the continued preservation of the most important parts of what they had inherited.

That being said, the conscious awareness of the need to preserve the physical patrimony and the resultant concrete steps to protect it are both fairly recent. The formal recognition of the house and chapel as historical monuments with protected status was granted in 1953; for the almshouses in 1974.

However, the Adornes history is much more than a story of bricks and mortar. It is also a story about people of flesh and blood. With her elegant pen and lively style, Véronique Lambert leads us through the hopes and fears, joys and sorrows, trials and tribulations that mark the milestones in the Adornes family saga. Within the boundaries of historical interpretation and based on extensive research, this much respected historian unfolds a fascinating tale of ambitious adventurers, charismatic personalities, flamboyant lords and ordinary mortals, but each imbued with the family's traditional willpower and energy.

In this account of high academic merit, Véronique Lambert has accurately brought to life the spirit of the times and the formidable passion and determination that inspired the main protagonists throughout the different centuries. For this, we are most grateful to her.

Countess Véronique de Limburg Stirum

In my eyes, Genoa is the most illustrious and most beautiful of all Italian cities. Perhaps I am being influenced and misled by my feelings for my distant ancestor, Opicino Adornes, who was born in Genoa, but I cannot remember that I have ever seen a city of such pleasing appearance, except perhaps Damascus.

(Jan Adornes, 1471)

FROM ADORNO TO ADORNES

Italian immigrants in Bruges

Just imagine: a migrant comes to our country and prospers so successfully that within a few generations his descendants are fabulously wealthy, occupy key political positions and are trusted at the highest level in matters of diplomacy. If it happened today, the newspapers would run out of superlatives to praise this outstanding example of cultural assimilation. The society magazines would be falling over each other to report on the doings of this new and influential dynasty. They would be hailed as role models for what can be achieved through hard work and integration; as an inspiration for everyone who wishes to seek fame and fortune away from their native land; as a source of encouragement for all those who believe that no ambition is too great as long as you are convinced in your own mind that it is possible.

The unlikely scenario is precisely what happened to the Adornes family. Their name was respected like few others in 15th century Bruges, where they not only had huge commercial interests but were also trendsetting figures in local society, enjoying great political prestige and with a direct line to the ruling dukes of Burgundy. Yet it was only a few decades previously that the founder of the family line had arrived in Flanders from Italy.

This first Adornes in Bruges must have been a man of many remarkable qualities. But who was he, exactly, this extraordinary person whose descendants quickly grew to become key decision-makers in what was then one of the most influential and prosperous cities in Northern Europe?

We actually know very little about him, but of two things we can be certain. He came from Genoa and his name was Opicino. This information comes from a travelogue written in 1471 by Jan Adornes (born 1444),

■ **The Adornes family originated from Genoa. Anselm
and Jan visited the city in 1470, during their journey
to Jerusalem.**
Christoforo de Grassi, View of Genoa. *1597, after a
drawing from 1481. Genoa, Galata Museum of the Sea.*

son of Anselm. On his way back from a pilgrimage to Jerusalem, Jan recorded: *That same day* [28 March 1470] *we arrived in Genoa, the city where the distant roots of our family are to be found, through Opicino Adorno, the great-great-grandfather of my father, who left Genoa and came with his wife to Bruges, where he is buried in the Abbey of the Poor Clares in a tomb that still exists. This Opicino had a son, Maarten, who is buried in the Chapel of the Friars Minor of the Dry Tree. Maarten and his wife, from the Schinkel family, in turn had a son, Peter, who became a great man in his own day.* Jan completed the family genealogy by adding the names of Peter and Anselm, his own father and grandfather.

Members of Opicino's Genoese family, who were known and respected as bankers and merchants, had been in contact with Flanders for a number of decades. It was sometime around 1320 that Opicino left his native city and travelled north with his Italian wife on one of the many Genoese galleys that regularly sailed to the port of Sluis, the outer harbour of Bruges. And it was in Bruges that Opicino eventually settled, attracted by the many opportunities offered by one of Europe's leading commercial and financial centres. It was here that he laid the foundations for his family's amazing success story.

■ In this miniature (ca. 1260) Guy of Dampierre is depicted as the Second Horseman of the Apocalypse: War. The Count of Flanders is recognizable from the black lion on his golden battledress.
Cambrai, Bibliothèque municipale, Ms. 422, fol. 20.

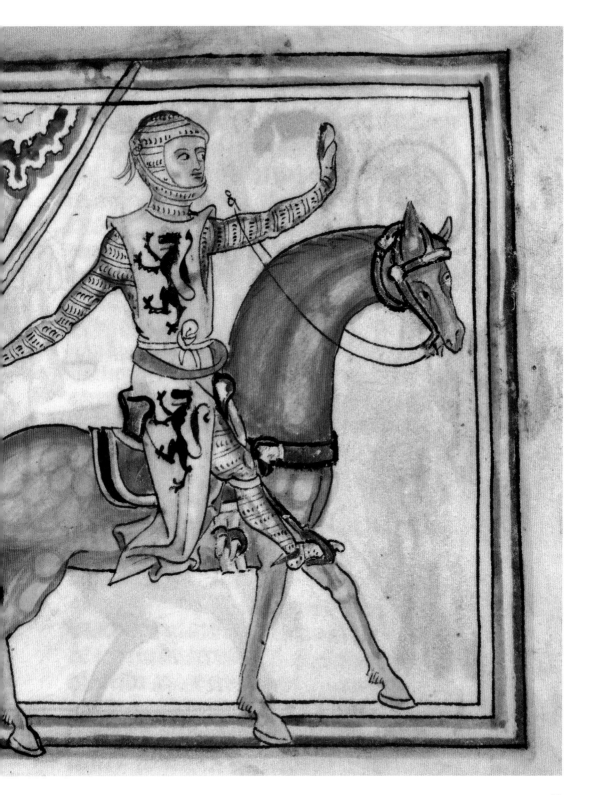

A little fantasy

In the 16th century, some 300 years after Opicino, another Adornes decided to write down the family history. As a scion of such a distinguished house, he felt obliged to 'create' a family tree that did justice to the power and prestige attached to the Adornes name. In those days, an influential family needed to have an influential founding father. For this reason - without batting a literary eyelid and without a shred of evidence - the writer linked his family name to the Crusades and to the court of the Count of Flanders at the end of the 13th century. His story begins on 12 April 1270. On that day, Guy of Dampierre, Count of Flanders, set off from his castle at Male with a large army of his retainers for the south of France. The knights were accompanied by a huge retinue of squires, falconers, cooks and messengers, since the expedition promised to be a long and difficult one. Passing first through Flanders and the County of Namur, the column wound its way through France, before finally arriving at the Mediterranean coast, where it was met by King Louis IX of France with his own troops. Guy was Louis' vassal and therefore had to obey the orders of the French king, who now commanded him to take part in a crusade to liberate the holy city of Jerusalem and the sacred tomb of Christ from Muslim occupation. As a preliminary, however, it was decided to first capture the port of Tunis, since Tunisian pirates were terrorizing the North African coast and blocking the sea routes to Palestine.

Sadly, the siege turned into a disaster. By now it was July and the European army, trapped on a flat desert plain under a blazing summer sun, began to slowly wither away. There was a shortage of drinking water and the French had only brought salted food with them, which made the problem of thirst even more acute. Dysentery and fever were soon rife, further thinning the ranks of the besiegers day by day. King Louis was among the victims, dying on 25 August 1270. Fortunately, the Flemish contingent was spared the worst effects of drought and disease. Guy had had the good sense to bring along supplies of wine, peas, barley, flour and herbs for his troops, as well as providing a doctor and a well-supplied chest of medicines. As a result, when the siege was finally lifted, most the Flemish noblemen and their retinues were able to return home in relative good health.

However, the cost of the expedition was enormous. The army had been away for more than a year, with all the expenditure this entailed for travel, lodging, victualing and soldiers' pay. Count Guy had little option but to borrow money to cover these costs, for which he turned to the services of merchants and bankers. Tradition says that a man from Genoa named Opicino Adornes was one of Guy's travel companions. Some argue that the Italian was so favoured by the count that he appointed him as his chamberlain. Others say that Opicino had lent the count such a huge sum of money that he joined the expedition simply to safeguard his investment. Once in Flanders, Opicino married Agnes, daughter of Philip of Axpoele, one of Guy's knights, and the couple had three children. The founder of the Adornes family line died in 1307 and was buried in St. Peter's Abbey in Ghent. His son, also named Opicino (or Opicinus), established himself in Bruges, where he married Margaret of Aartrijke. Their only son, Maarten, thereafter continued the family line.

Regrettably, there is no documentary evidence to support this fine-sounding story. The accounts for the Tunis expedition have survived and are very detailed, but they make no reference to an Opicino among the count's retinue. It therefore seems almost certain that this impressive family history was fabricated to match - and further boost - the family's already illustrious reputation. This does not mean that the Adornes were no more than self-glorifying liars. They simply did the same as every other leading family of the day - they used a little fantasy to create a story of what might have happened that was in keeping with their position as prominent members of society. What's more, their story was actually credible. Many later members of the Adornes family did indeed serve the counts of Flanders and they shared a great veneration for the holy places in Palestine. So why not Opicino as well?

Bruges is the most refined city in the world. It is with good reason that people say it is filled with all God's virtues and must be regarded as one of the most beautiful trading cities ever seen. The city is part of the sweet province of Flanders. Even though the soil is largely infertile, the sea and the foreign merchants make it one of the richest of cities in all respects, after Ghent, which is the first city and capital of Flanders. Because of its location and its beauty, it would be difficult to find a city that can compare to Bruges, the place that is our home.

(Jan Adornes, 1471)

BRUGES: VIBRANT TRADING METROPOLIS

In the early 14th century, France was the most populous country in Western Europe, with an estimated ten to fifteen million inhabitants. And the county of Flanders was the most populous region. As a result of their continuous growth, the cities were becoming increasingly powerful. Paris was the largest, with around 90,000 citizens, but was followed in second position by Ghent, whose 60,000 or so souls made it as large as London at that time. Bruges had an equally impressive 45,000 residents, making it the second most important urban centre in Flanders and a city of European importance.

Even so, the history of Bruges during this period was far from untroubled. The city militias - not professional soldiers, but ordinary citizens who knew how to handle a weapon - were repeatedly called into action during the war between France and Flanders which raged from 1297 to 1305, fighting in the bloody victory at the Battle of the Golden Spurs(1302) and in the equally bloody Battle of Pevelenberg (1304). The city had scarcely recovered from the horrors of this conflict when it was hit by famine in 1316, during which many thousands of people starved to death. Less than thirty years later, the population was decimated again, this time by the Black Death (although losses were less severe than in surrounding countries). Yet in spite of these disasters and an unstable social and political climate, Bruges was still able to flourish economically in the 14th and 15th centuries, eventually becoming the richest city in Flanders.

The city's direct link with the North Sea was crucial for this development. European merchants no longer made the tedious, expensive and dangerous overland journey to the annual fairs in the Champagne region. Maritime transport was safer, but was only financially viable for expensive goods with a high profit margin. For this

17

reason, the Flemish textile industry began to specialize in luxury products. The trade in these products was concentrated around ports and the location of Bruges, half way along the main sea routes between northern and southern Europe, gave the city a huge competitive advantage. Wide cogs from Germany and sleek galleys from Genoa and Venice sailed into the ports at Sluis or Damme, from where their cargoes were carried by barge along the canal to the centre of Bruges.

Goods that were imported in this manner through the Zwin inlet had to be sold by law in the city. To facilitate this, merchants from all over Europe were granted privileges and concessions by the city administration. The Italians imported Oriental spices, Iberian oil, Greek wine, rice and dyes, and on the return journey exported English wool and Flemish cloth to the Mediterranean. The Germans brought in Rhenish wine, beer, cod, rye and Russian fur, taking back figs, almonds, raisins and

spices, which they then sold throughout the Baltic region. The English and the Scots traded wool in the city's many halls and warehouses. The Portuguese specialized in sugar from Madeira and ivory and spices from Africa, while their Spanish neighbours from Castile concentrated on iron ore and wine from Poitou.

All these foreigners needed a place to eat, drink and sleep. They needed places to store their goods and local contacts to help sell them. They needed financial services to exchange foreign currencies and conduct business transactions in safety. Little wonder, therefore, that people in Bruges welcomed this 'invasion' with open arms. Local inns and taverns provided lodgings for foreign merchants, stables for their horses and storage space for their wares. The more commercially minded soon began serving as representatives, go-betweens, agents, guarantors and even as bankers, ensuring the smooth methods of payment that were necessary to oil the wheels of trade.

The streets of Bruges were bursting with the activity of butchers, fishmongers, bakers, tailors, cobblers, furriers, hosiers, milliners, glove makers and craftsmen of many other descriptions. The goldsmiths' stalls on the Burg sold jewellery of the very highest quality. Barrels of the finest French wine were unloaded at the Kraanrei, where its quantities were checked by monks from the St. John's Hospital, using an official measuring rod. The great city crane was operated by the so-called 'crane chil-

■ **Page 16-17. Thanks to this detailed map of Bruges, drawn by Marcus Gerards, we have a good idea of what the city looked like in the 16th century.**
Coloured copy of the map by Marcus Gerards, 1561. Bruges, Groeninge Museum. © www.lukasweb.be - Art in Flanders vzw foto Hugo Maertens, Dominique Provost.

■ **Trade goods were brought by small barges to the centre of the city, where they were unloaded.**
Miniature portraying the unloading of grain. 15th century. Ghent, St. Bavo's Cathedral, Ms. 10, fol. 71 v. © www.lukasweb.be - Art in Flanders vzw foto Hugo Maertens, Dominique Provost.

20

■ **The direct link with the North Sea played a crucial role in the development of Bruges as an international trading metropolis.**
Jan de Hervy, Map of the Zwin region. *16th century. Bruges, Groeninge Museum.*
© *www.lukasweb.be - Art in Flanders vzw foto Hugo Maertens, Dominique Provost.*

dren' and the necessary duty was collected by a legion of customs officers. Boats loaded with wool and cloth docked at the Water Hall on the Market Square, where the precious fabric was stored on the first floor and traded on the ground floor. An exception was made for the Scots and the English, whose merchandise was unloaded and weighed at the Engelsestraat. Corn arrived at the Groenerei and was sold at the Braamberg (the site of the present-day Fish Market). At each bridge and square, there was an army of porters waiting to carry anything that needed to be carried. Teams of horses pulled sledges that delivered wine and oil throughout the city. Basket-carriers shouldered loads of fresh fish to the waiting stalls on the Market Square.

Before long, exchange offices began to spring up in the vicinity of the various trading halls. On the square in front of the inn run by the Van der Beurse family, the Italians began to organize a daily financial market, where information was shared, currency rates noted and bills of exchange transacted.

For entertainment, there were the archery guilds of St. George and St. Sebastian or the plays and poetry readings performed by the so called 'chambers of rhetoric'. Other arts flourished under the patronage of the clergy and wealthy patricians, who commissioned richly illustrated manuscripts and paintings. Equally wealthy bankers encouraged the musical arts, hiring singers to amuse their guests with the popular polyphonic melodies of the day. Bathhouses such as 'In den Vulenbras' or 'Het Besemkin' were famed not only for their excellent food and bathing facilities, but also for more carnal attractions provided by 'attendants' such as *Nathalie die scone vrouwe* ('the beautiful Nathalie') and her colleagues.

Masons, tilers, plumbers and plasterers built monumental churches and elegant mansions, which were then lavishly decorated by local furniture makers, carpet weavers, smiths, carpenters and sculptors. The foreign merchants set up their own 'nation houses' or embassies, while the city's own wealth was reflected in the construction of the magnificent Late Gothic Town Hall and the proliferation of religious buildings, whose many towers (there were no fewer than six parish churches and seventeen monasteries within the old city walls) dominated the skyline.

■ The commercial heart of Bruges. Detail
from the map by Marcus Gerards, 1561.

Of course, not everyone prospered to the same extent. Like any big city, Bruges had its proletariat. And like most proletariats, it was crippled by poverty. The slum areas of the city were a maze of stinking, narrow alleys in the shadow of the outer city wall, where thousands of poor workers lived with their families. Many were day labourers, who hung around on the city's markets and squares in the hope of finding work. But often there was not enough work to go around, so that they wandered through the streets in a desperate search for food and money. Violence and crime were commonplace and small incidents could sometimes lead to larger outbreaks of disorder, which quickly degenerated into general plundering and wanton destruction. Needy pilgrims, travellers, traders, pedlars and beggars were sometimes able to find shelter in one of the city's hospices. If they were lucky, the old, the sick and the destitute were given places in an almshouse.

It was in this vibrant Bruges, in this ever turbulent trading metropolis on the threshold of the most golden period in its history that the fascinating epos of the Adornes family begins.

■ **The Kraanplein in Bruges can be seen in the background of this painting.**
Anonymous, Portrait of Filips Dominicile. *16th century. Bruges, Groeninge Museum. © www.lukasweb.be - Art in Flanders vzw foto Hugo Maertens, Dominique Provost.*

The decades during which the first Adornes is believed to have arrived in Bruges were particularly tumultuous. It was a time of almost constant social and political unrest. The counts of Flanders watched with increasing displeasure as the power of the cities continued to grow, threatening to undermine their traditional authority. The counts tried to control the rebellious cities by appointing aldermen who were favourable to them, but this could only ever be a stop-gap measure. Fortunately, they found a willing ally in the king of France. It was also in his best interests that the wealthy cities of Bruges, Ghent and Ypres should remain under the control of his vassal, especially since a more potent international conflict had broken out: the Hundred Years' War between France and England. This was a struggle for nothing less than the mastery of Europe and it was inevitable that Flanders - and therefore Bruges - would be drawn into the hostilities. The king of England naturally took offence that the counts of Flanders sided with the French cause simply to maintain their own position. As a result, the English responded by imposing a savage wool blockade. This hit the Flemish cloth workers very hard, since they were almost totally reliant on English wool for their livelihood. Social tension mounted, fuelled by growing unemployment and a shortage of grain. The demand for some form of political representation for the trades in the administration of the cities was loud and persistent. The result was a series of brutal rebellions. It was not until 1382 that some form of social stability was restored, with the count once again in the most powerful position. He finally and irrevocably won the right to appoint the aldermen in the cities and used this opportunity to create a pro-comital commercial elite that would henceforth do his bidding. This created the perfect conditions in which an ambitious family - like the Adornes - could climb their way to the top of the social hierarchy.

THE ADORNES IN BRUGES: THE CLIMB TO THE TOP

Maarten Adornes: the top is in sight

It was roughly half way through the 14th century when the name of one *Maertin Dadourne* or Maarten Adornes first began to appear in public records in Bruges. He was listed as being the 'lessee of the comital toll' in Damme. This meant that in return for the payment of a substantial sum of money the Count of Flanders granted him the right to collect all tolls in the port town of Damme - a win-win situation for both parties. For Count Louis of Male, it meant that he could avoid the need to employ an expensive official and also received a guaranteed source of income into the bargain. For Maarten, it meant that he could set the level of the tolls and impose their collection in such a way that he could make a significant profit. His appointment to this position makes clear that he was already a wealthy man and that he had close con-nections with the count's court. This was confirmed when he was later appointed as head of the St. John's quarter in Bruges, effectively making him burgomaster in one of the city's six districts within the walls. He now belonged to the city elite and as befitted his standing took up residence in an impressive mansion in the prosperous area bounded by the Cross Gate, the Langestraat and the Hoogstraat, St. John's Square and the Carmersstraat. He further cemented his position by marrying into the local patrician class, choosing as his bride a member of the influential Schinkel family, who provided several of the city's aldermen during the period 1334 to 1340. Maarten died in 1361 and was buried in the monastery chapel of the Friars Minor, close to the Braamberg.

Pieter I Adornes: the top is reached

Pieter Adornes, son of Maarten, started his career as an innkeeper. His inn - 'Ter Baerse' in the Vlamingstraat - was excellently located in the heart of the commercial district, between the Beurs and Market Squares, not far from the city's great crane. He was also the owner of 'De Witte Poorte' (Jan van Eyckplein 6) and 'Het Groot Galjoen' (Spinolarei 9), both close to the Toll House and the Burghers' Lodge. He used his hostels to provide accommodation and storage space for foreign merchants. And it was at his wine tables that deals were struck and letters of credit were exchanged. Profiting from this situation, the innkeeper gradually transformed himself into a broker and then a banker, before finally setting up an exchange house at St. Peter's Bridge, next to the 'De Matte' mansion (at the start of the present-day Philipstockstraat). He negotiated commercial deals with Englishmen, Easterners and Italians, soon becoming a pivotal figure in the international trade scene in Bruges. By now, he was a member of the patriciate, the city's highest social class. This was the group from which the members of the city administration were appointed and it was only logical that Pieter moved into politics. Before the end of his career, he served as head of the Carmer district, counsellor, alderman and burgomaster. As city treasurer, he reduced the level of public debt and restored the city's finances to some form of health.

Pieter married Margaret of Themseke, a daughter from an influential family of Bruges butchers. After her death, he remarried, this time choosing Elisabeth van de Walle as his new bride. The Van de Walles were an old patrician family, who had dominated the Bruges magistracy for decades and had provided the city with several aldermen. Both marriages marked the definitive acceptance of the Adornes family into the patrician class and gentlemen of standing were pleased to be invited to the home of *Her Pieter Adoren*, where *zanghers ende vedelaers* (singers and violinists) entertained the guests at dinner.

However, the ambitions of Pieter went much further than the local level. His father had maintained close ties with Count Louis of Male and Pieter now did the same with Louis' successor, Philip the Bold, Duke of Burgundy, who became Count of Flanders

■ In the city centre, merchants sold their wares in the various halls and markets. Here, a cloth merchant is showing a selection of buttons to a customer, while a shoemaker holds out his hand to receive payment for his services. The seller of crockery seems to be doing a roaring trade.
Miniature from a master associated with the workshop of Simon Marmion (probably the young Loyset Liédet). Ca. 1454. Rouen, Municipal Library, Ms. 1, 2(927), fol. 145.

■ Page 30. Barrels of wine were unloaded on the Kraanplein (Crane Square). The 'crane children' are operating the treadmill. The contents of the barrels were checked for both quantity and quality. A horse-drawn wagon is ready to provide transport.
Miniature by Simon Bening. 16th century. Munich State Library, Clm 23638, fol. 11 v.

■ The company of the *Witte Beer* (White Bear) held its
meetings in the Burgher's Lodge. Jacob, Pieter II and Anselm
Adornes were members of this prestigious jousting club.
Detail from Gerard David, The Judgement of Cambyses. *16th
century. Bruges, Groeninge Museum. © www.lukasweb.be - Art
in Flanders vzw foto Hugo Maertens, Dominique Provost.*

in 1384 following his marriage to Margaret of Male. Pieter concluded trade agreements on behalf of the duke and also travelled to Paris to buy luxury goods. His financial and diplomatic skill did not go unnoticed at the ducal court and in 1394 he was appointed as receiver-general for Flanders and Artois, one of the most important financial positions in all Burgundy and clear evidence of the duke's confidence in him.

Joris, Pieter II and Jacob Adornes: power and wealth

Pieter I had three sons: Joris from his first marriage, Pieter II and Jacob from his second union. They all soon followed in their father's footsteps. Joris took over the running of the exchange house and further expanded the family's commercial activities. Pieter II became collector of the city's excise duties. Jacob distinguished himself in the alum trade. Alum is a mineral used to fix the colouring of cloth and make the fabric light and water resistant. As such, it was an indispensible product for the manufacture of top-quality Flemish cloth, as well as having subsidiary applications in tanning and the glass industry. Given this context, it is not surprising that trade in alum became one of the family's most important sources of income.

Like their father, Jacob and Pieter II were also active in the political life of their native city. Jacob in particular profiled himself as a loyal patrician, who supported the ducal authority through thick and thin. In 1430, he even took part in the duke's military expedition against the rebellious peasants of Kassel. He was also head of the Carmer district when unrest once again broke out in Bruges in 1436. The city administration was still dominated by the wealthy burgher class, but the city's craftsmen were far from happy. A treaty concluded the previous year by Philip the Good with the French had led to new hostilities with England, which once again had a negative impact on the trade in wool and cloth. The situation was compounded by further disagreements with Sluis and the disruption of trade with the German Hanseatic League. The craft guilds met on the Market Square and declared what was effectively a general strike. Tempers flared and in the resulting scuffle the city's bailiff was killed. In panic, the city administrators fled and the craftsmen set up a revolutionary council. Jacob Adornes repeatedly attempted to mediate between both sides, in the hope of reconciling the townspeople to the duke's authority. This almost cost him

■ Even though crossbowmen are depicted, this is unmistakeably the practice ground of the Bruges St. Sebastian's Guild (archers), with the Cross Gate and the 'Bonne Chière' mill in the background. This practice ground was on land that was originally part of the Adornes domain, but was gifted by Pieter II to the guild. It is now the site of the Guido Gezelle Museum and home of the St. George's Archery Guild.
Miniature by Simon Bening. Ca. 1500. Brussels, Albert I Royal Library, Ms. II 158, fol. 11 v.

33

Prætorium

■ **The Jerusalem Chapel and the Adornes domain in
the 17th century.**
Antonius Sanderus, Flandria Illustrata, *1641, Vol. I,
p. 163. Universiteitsbibliotheek Gent (Ghent University
Library), BIB.G.005840.*

Ecclefia
Hierofolÿmæ
BRUGENSIS.

...iæ Adorniorum

his life. On 1 April 1437, he was attacked by an angry tailor and it was only thanks to the intervention of bystanders that he was not killed. Undeterred, he decided to remain in the city and continue his efforts to negotiate a settlement, even though the atmosphere was becoming increasingly hostile by the day. This was confirmed just weeks later, when the burgomaster and his brother were lynched by a mob. Jacob witnessed the attack and wanted to intervene, armed only with a hammer, and had to be prevented by his friends from risking his life pointlessly. He now had little option but to go into hiding. After the duke reasserted his authority, Philip rewarded Jacob for his unconditional loyalty in 1438 by appointing him as burgomaster of Bruges and he continued to occupy leading civil functions until his death in 1465.

Pieter II and Jacob Adornes: an aristocratic lifestyle

By the start of the 15th century, the Adornes family belonged to the very highest circles of Bruges society. Their trading and financial activities had helped them to amass a considerable fortune. Their unfailing support for the duke had opened the door to high political office, both in Bruges and at the ducal court. Advantageous marriages had created ties of blood with the city's other leading patrician families. In short, their prestige and power were now firmly rooted in both city and county. But the final accolade still eluded them: they were not yet regarded as members of the aristocracy. As a preliminary to taking this final step up the social ladder, both Pieter II and Jacob began to adopt an overtly aristocratic lifestyle.

Both brothers were members of the *Witte Beer* (White Bear) jousting club, a setting which allowed the top of the Bruges magistracy to measure themselves against the scions of the Flemish and Burgundian nobility, whilst also clearly demonstrating their 'knightly' aspirations. As a young man, Pieter II was something of a club favourite as the *forestier*, the organiser of the annual tournament in Bruges. He also regularly took part in other tournaments in Brussels and Lille.

At the same time, Jacob worked himself up to become head of the prestigious St. Sebastian's archery guild. Pieter II was not a member of the guild, but nonetheless gifted it a large piece of land on the Rolweg with *husen en muren* (houses and walls), which the archers used as their premises and practice ground.

The Adornes family also threw itself with vigour into the world of culture and art. Around 1450, Pieter II and his wife, Elisabeth Braderic, commissioned a portrait from the celebrated painter Petrus Christus and they also had good contacts with Jan van Eyck. The brothers also collected an extensive library of books, which included classical authors like Virgil and Cicero, but

also humanist writers such as Lorenzo Valla, the Florentine historian Leonardo Bruni and the poet Francesco Petrarch, as well as bibles, theological books, anatomical texts and treatises on astronomy and geography. In 1452, Pieter II and his wife even unveiled a plan to open a kind of public library in the family chapel. *All our books, both Latin and Flemish, must be placed on lecterns in the Jerusalem Chapel, the Latin books on the right and the Flemish books on the left, so that everyone can read them.* This was no collection of luxuriously illustrated manuscripts, such as those held in the library of Louis of Gruuthuse, but was one of the earliest collections of humanist works, with attention for ancient literature, history, science and poetry. During the 20th century, this earned the family fame as 'the most important secular humanists' in medieval Bruges.

Yet for all their interest in humanist ideas, religious devotion was unquestionably a cornerstone in the public and private lives of the Adornes family. Jacob was a member of the Brotherhood of Our Lady of the Dry Tree, while the name of Pieter II can be found among the membership lists of no fewer than nine religious fraternities, to all of which he bequeathed a legacy in his will. He even received permission from no less a person than the pope to celebrate mass at his own portable altar in his mansion in the Peperstraat and he also enjoyed the exceptional (and aristocratic) privilege of having his own father confessor. After his wife died in 1452, Pieter II withdrew from public life and a few years later entered the

Valley of Mercy monastery of the strict Carthusian Order (although he followed a less rigorous regime than the monks).

All the Adornes had a strong sense of veneration for the Holy Places. According to tradition, Pieter II and Jacob once made a pilgrimage to the Holy Land, although there is no real evidence to support this claim. We know that Jacob certainly made plans for a pilgrimage to Rome in 1449, but we have no further information about this trip. What we certainly do know is that the brothers built a chapel alongside Pieter's house in the Peperstraat, dedicated to 'the Passion of Christ and the Holy Sepulchre'. In 1427, Pope Martin V gave his permission for a clock tower to be erected alongside this Jerusalem Chapel in brick, a material that was usually reserved exclusively for parish churches. A chaplain performed a daily mass in the chapel, which the beguines living on the domain were required to attend. The family members were also given permission to be buried there, a guarantee that prayers for the benefit of their souls would be said throughout all eternity as their personal key to the gates of the heavenly Jerusalem.

■ These postcards from 1925 are copies of an original copper engraving (ca. 1585-1634) by Peter de Jode the Elder, depicting Pieter II Adornes and his wife, Elisabeth Braderic. The engravings were possible based on an earlier painting of the couple made by Petrus Christus around 1450.
Beeldbank Brugge, FO/A01336. 'verz. J. A. Rau'.

ANSELM ADORNES: a remarkable man with a remarkable life

Sunday's child

On 8 December 1424, Elisabeth Braderic, the wife of Pieter II Adornes, gave birth to a child. Their joy knew no bounds. A son! And perfectly healthy! The continued existence of the family name was assured. In keeping with the custom of the time, the child was accompanied at the baptismal font by no fewer than three godfathers and two godmothers. The infant was named Anselm. At that moment, neither of the parents could have imagined what a remarkable life their first-born child would lead. Because Anselm was destined to be much more than just another face in the crowd.

The child grew up in the luxurious home of his parents in the domain on the corner of the Peperstraat and the Balstraat. As a toddler, he was allowed to help lay the first stone of the foundations for the Jerusalem Chapel, which his father had built alongside the family mansion. Little could anyone know that 50 years later Anselm would have it torn down.

The young boy received the best possible education. His native tongue was Middle Dutch, but his father also taught him Italian from an early age. In the parish school he learnt reading, writing, music and mathematics. He later went to the chapter school, probably at St. Donatian's. This was where most of the Bruges elite were educated. Here he studied Latin and was prepared for university. In 1438 - when he was just 14 years old! – he went to Leuven to follow the classes of Antonius Haneron, who was later the *maistre d'*école *et instituteur* at the court of Duke Philip the Good.

■ These sketches show us Anselm Adornes and his wife Margareta van der Banck. They are design drawings for statues that were originally intended to be placed above the entrance doors to the upper chapel, but were never made.
Adornes collection.

■ Interior of the medieval patrician mansion, following restoration.

Anselm was a bright lad: alert, smart, inquisitive, studious. He browsed through his father's books, watched how the merchants conducted their negotiations and familiarized himself with the various goods arriving at the Water Hall. As the child of rich parents during the golden age of Burgundian Bruges, he was able to experience the city's great events from the front row. At the annual fair, he marveled at the heroism of the jousting tournament. But he was equally enthralled by the concerts in honour of Our Lady given by the city musicians on the balcony of the belfry tower. And when the Holy Blood procession passed through the streets, he hung on his father's every word. Stories about the Passion of Christ fascinated him. During the masses he attended at the small Jerusalem Chapel, his fantasy took him to the Holy Places and the Holy Land would continue to intrigue him throughout his life.

In January 1430, the six-year-old Anselm witnessed the ceremonial entry of Isabella of Portugal into Bruges. The visiting duchess was carried through the city on a litter decorated with gold, ivory and brocade, mounted between two white horses with bridles made from silver and Cordoba leather, and followed by a colourful retinue of attendants and performers. There were celebrations throughout the town for a whole week and Duke Philip the Good formally announced the initiation of the knightly Order of the Golden Fleece. Two years later, an entranced Anselm watched the procession of the Fleece knights to St. Donatian's Church,

■ Duke Philip the Good was usually dressed in black. On his chest hangs the chain of the Order of the Golden Fleece, the prestigious knightly order he founded in Bruges in 1430.
After Rogier van der Weyden, Portrait of Philip the Good. *Second half of the 15th century. Bruges, Groeninge Museum. © www.lukasweb.be - Art in Flanders vzw foto Hugo Maertens, Dominique Provost.*

■ Right. Detail from the monumental tomb of Anselm Adornes and Margareta van der Banck. Margareta is wearing a fashionable hennin headdress.
Jerusalem Chapel.

dressed in their red capes and wearing their golden chains. His father explained that membership of the order was the highest honour the duke could bestow on a man. It was something that Anselm never forgot. Little by little, he was introduced to the codes and rituals that were a part of the patrician life he would be expected to lead. At the same time, his ambition was nurtured and encouraged. By the time he reached adulthood, Anselm would not be satisfied with anything less than the very highest positions of power and prestige.

His carefree childhood years came to an end in 1436, when the craftsmen of Bruges rose in rebellion against Duke Philip the Good. The city was ablaze and the Adornes family, well-known supporters of the duke, were in danger. Not wishing to take unnecessary risks, Pieter II led his family to the safety of the hinterland. It was another two years before famine and plague forced the rebels to their knees. The duke's repression was merciless. Ten of the rebel leaders were publically executed and their severed heads were fixed on spikes on the Cross Gate as a warning to others who might think of challenging the ducal authority. When Anselm returned to Bruges with his parents, they passed under the Gate where the duke's revenge was still all too patently evident. The twelve-year-old youth immediately understood that this was the price to be paid by those who were not loyal to those in power. It was a lesson he would remember for the rest of his days.

Once back in the city, things continued to prosper for the Adornes family. Pieter further prepared his son for the life he would lead in the highest circles of Bruges society and occasionally took him to the *Prinsenhof* (Prince's Court), the ducal residence in Bruges. Anselm had already learnt French, the language of the court, and he closely followed the preparations of the city authorities for the so-called 'joyous entry' of Philip the Good into Bruges in 1440. He was also to be found increasingly in and around the town hall, where the polychrome images of past dukes and counts on the gable further stimulated his ambition. The social and political networks of his father and uncle were the ideal platform for the almost limitless aspirations of this very talented young man.

A political animal

Anselm was not yet nineteen years old when he married the three years younger Margareta vander Banck, daughter of another leading patrician family. It was also about this time that he made his entry into public life and began his political career. Starting as a counsellor, he climbed his way up to become the head of the St. John and St. Nicholas quarters, city treasurer and finally city burgomaster. His other important functions included guardianship of the Lepers' House and a position as a governor of the *Proosse* (enclave) of St. Donatian.

■ Anselm Adornes, in full armour, and a lavishly dressed Margareta van der Banck kneel in prayer. Behind them stand their patron saints, St. Anselm and St. Margaret. The chain of the Order of the Unicorn is draped around Anselm's coat of arms, surmounted by his motto Para tutum. The sunburst clouds and the Cross of Jerusalem are also prominent.
Jerusalem Chapel.

A captain of industry

Like his grandfather, Anselm distinguished himself in international commerce. He imported alum and traded in cloth from Tournai and England. He also acted as an intermediary for foreign merchants, particularly those from Genoa and Spain.

His impressive residence on the Ververs-dijk, directly opposite the Stokvisbrug (close to the present-day Sint-Anna-kerkstraat) was part of a larger industrial complex of cellars, warehouses, galleries, stables, an inn and three dyeing workshops. These workshops specialized in the colouring of loose wool and finished cloth. Dyeing was a complex and time-consuming task. Huge copper tubs were hung above furnaces half dug into the ground, in which the dyers brought the fabric to the boil in a mixture of salt and water. Alum was then added to open the fibres of the wool, so that the colouring would be more firmly fixed. A few days later, the colouring plants would be added to the tubs: madder for red, woad for blue and rocket for yellow. The solution was then carefully brought to the boil again, stirring all the time. Finally, the coloured cloth was washed in hot water. This entire process was subject to strict rules. The amount of colorant, its quality, the mordant, the number of times the colour bath could be used, the quantity of wool or cloth that could be coloured at the same time: all these things were carefully prescribed and monitored by the dyers' guild.

A networker

More than any of his contemporaries, Anselm understood that a good network was as crucial for success as hard work. As a result, he regularly frequented the circles and events where he could be sure of meeting other members of the Bruges *beau monde*.

■ **Two cloth dyers stir the contents of the dyeing tub, watched closely by a cloth merchant who is checking the quality of the dyeing process.**
Miniature from De proprietatibus rerum *by Bartholomaeus Anglicus. Bruges, 1482. London, British Library, Royal 15 E. III, fol. 269.*

The aristocratic *Witte Beer* jousting club, the Brotherhood of Our Lady of the Dry Tree, the St. Sebastian archers' guild: there was no prestigious society or association for gentlemen of standing to which Anselm did not belong. He systematically established contacts with influential people like Jan de Baenst (diplomat and adviser to Philip the Good and patron of writers and poets), the fabulously wealthy Jacob van der Beurse (banker and commercial agent) and Louis of Gruuthuse (bibliophile, patron of the arts, diplomat, counsellor and knight in the Order of the Golden Fleece). Prince Anthony of Burgundy, a bastard son of Duke Philip, was also among his friends, taking part no less than ten times in the *Witte Beer* tournament and acting as *sire* for the St. Sebastian's guild in 1463.

Anselm's desire to prove himself in these fora was boundless and pushed him to extremes. He was known as one of the most aggressive participants in the *Witte Beer* tournaments and on 1 May 1447 he organized his own tournament near the ponds of Male castle, where he challenged all-comers. Here he fought against Adolf of Kleve and the legendary Jacques de Lalaing, two leading nobles of the day, and two knights from Bruges, Eustachius Wyts and Cornelis Metteneye. During the joust, Anselm drove his lance so forcefully into Metteneye's helmet that it burst open, almost killing his opponent in what was supposed to be a 'friendly' match.

■ To mark the marriage of Charles the Bold and Margaret of York (1468) numerous feasts and celebrations were held in Bruges. Anselm Adornes organized the tournament on the market square.
Anonymous, Portrait of Margaret of York. *1468. Paris, Musée du Louvre. Département des peintures, R.F. 1938-17.*

■ Left. Jousting was one of the favourite sports of the elite. In this way, the Adornes could display their knightly aspirations. This miniature was painted in Bruges. In the background we can see the tower of the Jerusalem Chapel.
Miniature by Simon Bening. Ca. 1500. Brussels, Albert I Royal Library, Ms. II 158, fol. 6 v.

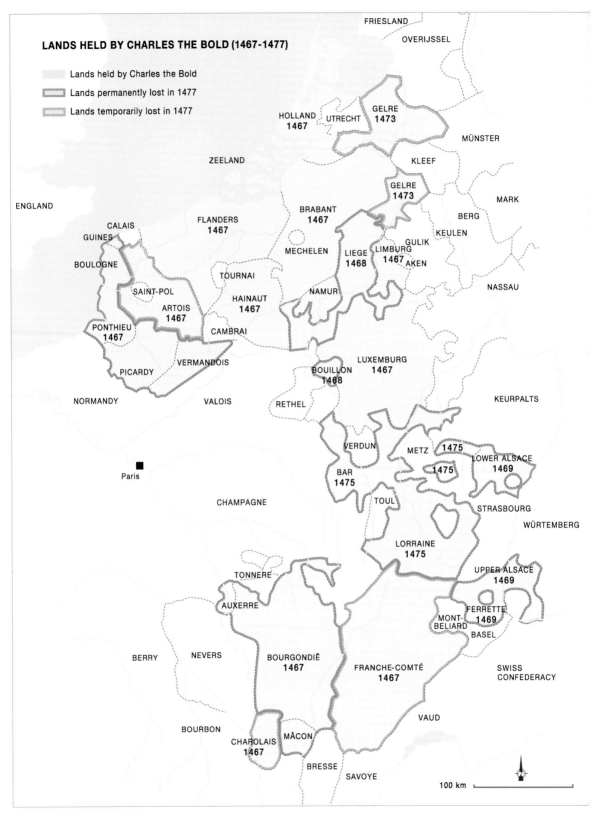

LANDS HELD BY CHARLES THE BOLD (1467-1477)

- Lands held by Charles the Bold
- Lands permanently lost in 1477
- Lands temporarily lost in 1477

FRIESLAND

OVERIJSSEL

GELRE
1473

HOLLAND
1467

UTRECHT

MÜNSTER

ZEELAND

KLEEF

GELRE
1473

MARK

ENGLAND

FLANDERS
1467

BRABANT
1467

BERG

KEULEN

CALAIS
GUINES

MECHELEN

LIEGE
1468

GULIK

LIMBURG
1467

AKEN

BOULOGNE

TOURNAI

NASSAU

SAINT-POL

HAINAUT
1467

NAMUR

ARTOIS
1467

PONTHIEU
1467

CAMBRAI

LUXEMBURG
1467

VERMANDOIS

BOUILLON
1468

PICARDY

KEURPALTS

NORMANDY

VALOIS

RETHEL

Paris

VERDUN

METZ 1475

1475

LOWER ALSACE
1469

CHAMPAGNE

BAR
1475

TOUL

STRASBOURG

WÜRTEMBERG

LORRAINE
1475

TONNERE

UPPER ALSACE
1469

AUXERRE

MONT-
BELIARD

FERRETTE
1469

BASEL

BERRY

NEVERS

BOURGONDIË
1467

FRANCHE-COMTÉ
1467

SWISS
CONFEDERACY

VAUD

BOURBON

MÂCON

CHAROLAIS
1467

BRESSE

SAVOYE

100 km

N

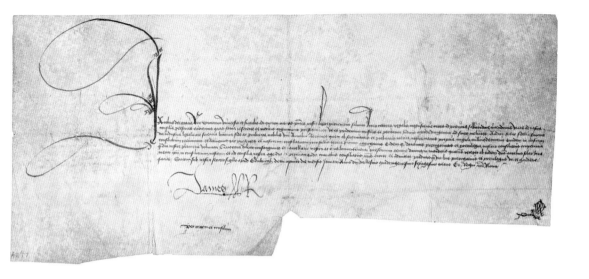

A loyal lieutenant

In keeping with his family tradition, Anselm Adornes proved himself to be a loyal supporter of the duke and maintained close contacts with the ducal court.

When Philip the Good died in Bruges on 15 June 1467, Anselm was one of the local notables who accompanied the funeral cortege to the burial service in the St. Donatian Church.

A year later, major celebrations were organized to mark the marriage of Philip's successor, Charles the Bold, to the English princess, Margaret of York. Anselm was given the honour of acting as the right-hand man of Anthony of Burgundy for the organisation of the celebratory tournament on the Market Square. And what a tournament it was! Inside the arena, they wore their most expensive armour and weapons. Outside the arena, the knights were dressed in their most luxurious embroidered garments of damask, silk or fine cloth, trimmed with mink or ermine, topped with colourful headgear decorated with bells and ostrich feathers., Each evening, after the day's combat, there was a spectacular banquet, complete with gaily decorated pheasants and peacocks, imitation animals bearing baskets of sweets and fruit, and even a fire-breathing dragon. But the apotheosis was the entry of a golden leopard riding on the back of unicorn, followed by a camel ridden by a Moor,

■ On 15 January 1469, King James III of Scotland appointed Anselm Adornes as one of his royal counsellors.
Bruges, City Archives, Archief Adornes, inv.nr. 24.

who distributed doves and partridges to the noblewomen assembled in the hall, while jugglers, dancers and musicians all plied their arts. Even Anselm, who was used to the very best that life could offer, hardly knew where to look first!

A talented diplomat

Anselm's residence was in a district of the city where primarily Scottish merchants were active. The Schottendijk (Scots' Dyke, the present-day Sint-Annarei) was just across the canal and the Schottenplaats (Scots' Square) was immediately behind the Adornes complex. As a true-blooded entrepreneur and networker, Anselm spared no effort to maintain good relations with his Scottish neighbours.

The Scots mainly trade in wool. However, when their king announced a trade embargo in 1467, they left the city. This was potentially a commercial disaster both for Bruges and for Flanders, and led to the summoning of the Four Members, a periodic meeting between the representatives of Bruges, Ghent, Ypres and the Franc of Bruges. The Four Members appealed to the ducal court at the highest level for assistance and in 1468 it was decided to send a diplomatic mission to Scotland. Because of his previous good contacts with the Scots, leadership of the mission was entrusted to Anselm, who at that time was also respon-

sible as treasurer for the city's finances. When he arrived at the court of King James III, he made an impassioned plea on behalf of the interests of Bruges and its importance as a hub of international commerce, in which he compared the city with the other great university cities of Europe, calling it 'the university of trade'. This emotional but well-reasoned appeal, put forward by an experienced diplomat dressed in his very best finery, made a strong impression on the frail young king, and during the long negotiations that followed friendship and mutual respect grew on both sides.

The mission was crowned with success. The king withdrew the embargo and the Scottish merchants returned to Bruges. Anselm's reputation as a negotiator was now at its zenith and his prestige soared to new and unprecedented heights. But his ultimate reward was still to come: his excellent relations with James III at long last opened the doors to ennoblement. The Scottish king made him a knight in the Order of the Unicorn, appointed him as a royal adviser, and granted him the manor of Cortachy.

■ James III regularly made use of
the talents of Anselm Adornes and
rewarded him handsomely for his
services. It was probably Anselm
who brought the king into contact
with Hugo van der Goes.

Hugo van der Goes, Portrait of
James III. *1478. Edinburgh, Scottish
National Gallery. Royal Collection
Trust/© Her Majesty Queen
Elizabeth II 2018.*

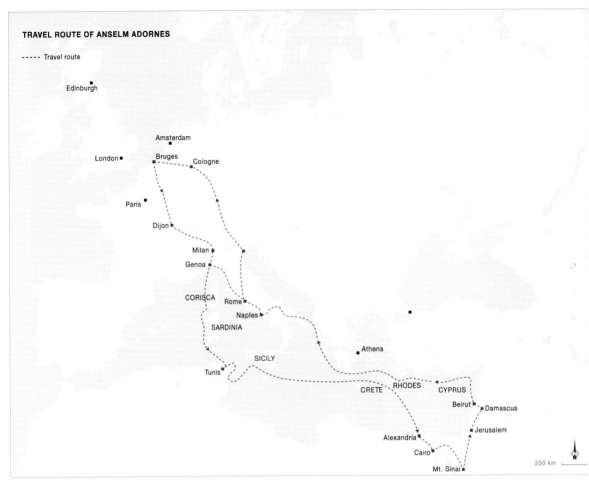

----- Travel route

Edinburgh

Amsterdam

London   Bruges   Cologne

Paris

Dijon

Milan

Genoa

CORISCA   Rome

Naples

SARDINIA

Athens

SICILY

Tunis

CRETE   RHODES   CYPRUS

Beirut   Damascus

Jerusalem

Alexandria

Cairo

Mt. Sinai

200 km

■ Right. In his first will, Anselm Adornes stipulated that his two sweet daughters, Margriete and Louise – both of whom were nuns in a convent – should each be given a painting depicting St. Francis of Assisi. These paintings were made by no less an artist then Jan van Eyck. It is not clear whether the portraits were ever given to Margriete and Louise, but they have survived and are now to be found in Turin and Philadelphia.
Jan van Eyck, St. Francis receives the stigmata. *Ca. 1435-40. Sabauda Gallery, Turin.*

A loyal friend

At the time of Anselm's stay in Scotland, the country was dominated by the powerful Boyd clan. The head of the clan, Robert Boyd, was even able to arrange for the marriage of his son, Thomas, to Mary, the sister of King James. However, a short time later the Boyds overstepped the mark once too often and fell into disgrace. Mary, Thomas and Robert were forced to leave

Scotland and they travelled to Flanders, where they hoped they could rely on the hospitality of Anselm and Margareta.

They were not disappointed: the Adornes welcomed them with open arms - an act that not only further increased the gratitude of King James towards Anselm, but also won him even greater prestige in his native city as the host to a foreign princess.

A devout adventurer

When Anselm Adornes began to make plans for a pilgrimage to Jerusalem around the year 1470, he was fully aware of the risks involved. The round journey to the Holy Land by horse and boat was more than 5,000 kilometres, a huge distance in those days and one fraught with danger every step of the way. Seventeen years after the fall of Constantinople in 1453, the Middle East was more than ever a highly volatile powder-keg, dominated by the persistent and virulent hate between Christians and Muslims. The Ottoman Empire was in the process of becoming one of the most powerful imperial regimes in the known world, with its territory stretching from south of the Danube to west of the Euphrates. The centuries of conflict between Christian Europe and militant Islam in the Mediterranean basin had helped to create a strong dislike of Westerners in large parts of North Africa and the Middle East. This meant that to reach Jerusalem Anselm would need to travel through strange lands and strange cultures that were potentially hostile. But that was not the only threat. The Black Death that had decimated Europe's population a century earlier was still raging in the Middle East, bringing with it the prospect of a slow and painful death.

But Anselm was not to be deterred. He was a deeply devout man and his family had a long tradition of veneration for the Holy Cross. A pilgrimage to the Holy Sepulchre would confirm and give public expression to the strength of his belief. As an added benefit, he could also visit family and friends and establish new diplomatic and commercial contacts along the way.

Mindful of the risks he was taking, Anselm made his last will and testament before his departure. He also gave detailed instructions for his eventual burial in the Jerusalem Chapel. These measures gave his family a degree of comfort and security, should he not return from his pilgrimage - which he knew was a real possibility. Clear-minded as ever, he weighed up the pros and cons and decided that he had to go: his faith demanded it.

In case things went wrong, he also took steps to safeguard his immortal soul. He gifted one hundred meals to the poor as penance for his sins. A further thousand paupers receive a loaf of bread and a silver coin. If he died en route without having confessed, he arranged for his sons to plead for his absolution from the pope in Rome. He also entreated all the local hospices, monasteries and churches in Bruges to pray for him, gifting them bolts of cloth in return for the saying of masses on his behalf. In this way, he hoped to limit his time in purgatory and enter through the gates of paradise with a minimum of delay!

It was February 1470 before Anselm's pilgrimage finally set off for Palestine. There were seven of them in the party: Anselm, his chamberlain, three other pilgrims and two other citizens of Bruges. After receiving confession and Holy Communion in the Jerusalem Chapel, they mounted their horses and headed south in the direction of Milan, some 1,200 kilometres away. This took them through Picardy, Artois, Champagne, Burgundy, Savoy and across the Alps. Less than 40 years after the burning of Joan of Arc in Rouen (1431), France was still attempting to recover from the devastating effects of the Hundred Years' War (1337-1453) with their arch-enemy England.

After four weeks they arrived safely in Milan on 20 March. Their reception was almost royal: hunting with the duke, guided tours of the city, banquets with local notables. After a month of hard travelling in the saddle, this was a welcome opportunity to rest and recuperate in accommodation that was something more than a village inn!

From Milan, they rode on to Pavia, where Anselm's oldest son, Jan, had already been studying for five years. He now decided to break off his studies, so that he could accompany the pilgrims on the rest of their journey. The group, now eight strong, set off for Genoa, the spiritual home of the Adornes family, before moving on to Pisa (10 April) and Rome, where they arrived on the Wednesday before Easter (18 April). In the larger cities, they were usually able to stay with family or friends, which gave them the opportunity to witness at first hand the amazing cultural revolution that was taking place in Italy and would soon transform Europe: the Renaissance. Their introduction to this ground-breaking movement in architecture, science, art and philosophy made a deep impression on the men from Bruges.

Adornes was a name that could open doors everywhere. In Rome, Anselm was granted several private audiences by no less a person than Pope Paul II, who gave his papal

·PAVLVS·II·PONT·MAX·

■ **Pope Paul II granted Anselm Adornes a number of private audiences.**
Cristofano dell'Altissimo, Portrait of Pope Paul II. *Second half of the 16th century. Florence, Galleria degli Uffizi.*

blessing for the pilgrimage to *the lands of the unbelievers* and granted forgiveness for all the sins committed by Anselm and his family, both in their lifetime and at the moment of their death. He even personally placed a consecrated Lamb of God medallion around Anselm's neck to provide holy protection against danger and disease during the remainder of his journey.

After celebrating Easter in Rome, Anselm and his group returned to Genoa, where he had previously booked five passages on a ship to Tunis. He deliberately chose not to follow the traditional pilgrim's route across the Mediterranean Sea from Venice to Jaffa (now part of Tel Aviv). His Genoese contacts had told him that these Venetian galleys were packed to overflowing with pilgrims in the most unhygienic conditions, which made them a perfect - and deadly - breeding ground for sicknesses of all kinds. The three other pilgrims from Bruges ignored this good advice and took their leave of Anselm's party, preferring nonetheless to make the voyage from Venice. It was to prove a fatal decision. More than half the passengers on their galley contracted disease on board, from which they later died before completing their journey.

Adornes father and son and their three remaining companions set sail for Tunis on 7 May in a Genoese carrack, a sturdy and seaworthy craft of the kind that would allow Christopher Columbus to make his voyage of discovery to America just 20 years later. The carrack offered the Bru-

ges pilgrims safety and comfort. It was equipped with bombards (an early type of cannon) and its hundred-man crew was more than capable of beating off any attacks by Turks or pirates. The cabins were spacious, there was plenty of opportunity to relax on deck and the food was good by the maritime standards of the day, with biscuits, sweets, pastries and wine all included on the menu. There was even a medicine chest with remedies to combat stomach cramps and headaches!

Having left Genoa on the evening tide to the sound of trumpets and a salute of cannons, favourable winds took the ship first to Corsica (12 May) and then to Sardinia (18 May),before making the last stretch of the crossing to Tunis, where they docked on 5 June. This was the first real moment of culture shock. Their initial experience of an unknown continent affected the Europeans deeply and they were repeatedly amazed by the strange local customs.

The men's clothes are wide and flowing, while their shoes are so long at the front that you could comfortably get two feet inside... The women in the street wear voluminous white cloaks that reach down to the ground, a little like those worn by our women, but these cover the entire face, so that only the eyes are visible... The arms and hands of both men and women are of-

■ One of the corner towers is decorated with a radiant sun, as a symbol for God.

ten painted and decorated with all different kinds of symbols. I don't understand how this decoration is applied, because it does not fade with washing or time. I suspect that it is burnt into the skin.

The Christian Anselm and his party were made welcome in the Islamic city of Tunis. Infact, they stayed there for nearly a whole month. They were present at the Muslim Feast of the Sacrifice and were received with respect at the royal palace. The king gave them a permit to explore the immediate vicinity of the city but warned them against going any further, since the roads were being terrorized by *Arabs and robbers* and many of the outlying villages were ravaged by plague. This persuaded Anselm to abandon any idea of making an overland journey and so he set sail by boat for the Egyptian port of Alexandria.

On arrival, they bought in supplies and hired two curious-looking beasts of burden, which local people told them were called 'camels'. They next engaged a reliable guide and a translator, so that by 2 August they were ready to set off on the long and difficult journey to Cairo. This was the hottest month of the year, and the men from Bruges soon found their confidence badly shaken by the harshness of the desert world of sand, wind, extreme temperatures, incomprehensible languages and unfamiliar cultural patterns. The last part of the journey was made by boat along the Nile and at one point they feared for their lives when they were forced to change from the small boat they had hired to a much larger vessel. They thought they were about to be sold to slave traders, but fortunately it was the only boat that had a monopoly on carrying passengers to Cairo. Even so, the rest of the journey was a horrific one. They were *treated as animals by the Moors* and the Mamluks were not afraid to use force to deprive their European passengers of their supply of wine.

It was with great relief that Anselm and his companions sailed into Cairo on 7 August. They made their way to the sultan's palace and asked to speak to one of his translators, in the hope of receiving some royal hospitality. They certainly received hospitality - they were allowed to stay in the palace for eight days - but it was anything but royal. The sultan charged them a small fortune for his 'generous' welcome and tried to swindle the pilgrims out of every last penny. Anselm was furious and instantly lost all faith in Egyptians, whether Christian or Muslim.

In spite of the clear hostility of the local people towards Western 'unbelievers', the group decided to take a look around the city. They were amazed by the monumental architecture of Ancient Egypt and astonished by the size of the pyramids at Giza. They even summoned up the courage to go inside!

■ Anselm and Jan Adornes brought back this Byzantine cross from his pilgrimage. The silver decoration was added later.
Adornes collection.

In the desert, there are a number of ancient monuments in the form of a pyramid. They are built from huge blocks of stone and their overall size is astounding. Some say that these were the granaries where grain was stored by the pharaoh during the seven years of plenty, so that it was possible to survive the seven lean years that followed. But we think that they are tombs, because the only entrance is a small doorway, behind which there is a dark and narrow passage that leads to a single chamber, but not a large hall.

On 15 August, the moment came for them to start the most treacherous leg of their journey: from Cairo to the Holy Land. But it was also one of the most religiously inspiring, making it possible to stop at sites like the place where Mary, Joseph and Jesus had lived during their stay in Egypt and the Red Sea where Moses had parted the waves to allow the Israelites to escape the vengeance of the pharaoh. Even so, the exhausting trek through the inhospitable desert was harsh in the extreme. In their travel dairy, the pilgrims paint a vivid picture of the trials and tribulations of this hellish voyage through a sea of sand and over outcrops of jagged rock under a burning sun. At last, on 24 August, they saw the outline of Mount Sinai in the distance and staggered into the sanctuary of the St. Catherine's Monastery, grateful to have reached this oasis of peace and safety unharmed.

On the right, next to the choir or the Holy of Holies, there is a small rectangular reliquary in white marble, in which the monks deposited the skull and the bones of St. Catherine, virgin and martyr, after finding her body in the mountains. The guardians with the three keys opened the sarcophagus and showed us with great pomp and pride the saint's mortal remains. All the monks were there and they each held a candle in their hand. They knelt in front of the remains and one by one they kissed the bones. After this, it was our turn to view the relics and kiss them twice. My father [meaning Anselm: it is his son Jan who is writing] *was given permission to bring his ring and jewels for the princes into contact with the bones. The brothers also laid a piece of silk on the bones, tore it in strips, and gave each of us a fragment.*

In the days that followed, the pilgrims - having first paid the prescribed toll to the guide - visited the many holy places in and around the monastery: the site of the burning bush, the spring which flowed from the rock where Moses struck his rod and all the holy places on Mount Sinai and Mount Catherine. Inspired by these sights by day, they spent less inspiring nights in the two cramped and primitive cells reserved by the monks for pilgrims, who were expected to sleep in all sobriety on the floor.

It was now time to push on to their final destination: Jerusalem. These last few hundred kilometres through hostile Ottoman territory were not without risk. For centuries, there had been tension between the Christian and Islamic worlds. Follow-

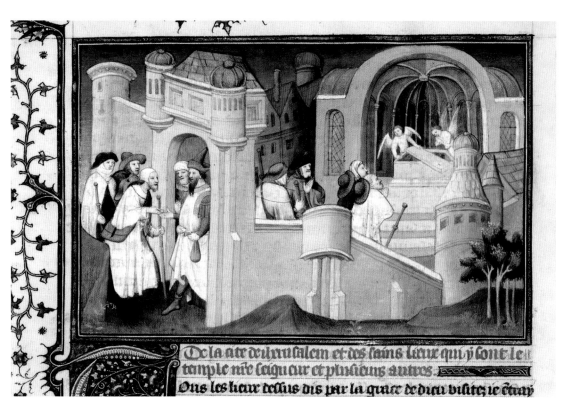

De la cite de Jherusalem et des sains lieux qui y sont le
temple nře seigneur et plusieurs autres.
Ous les lieux dessus dis par la grace de dieu visitez ie estoy

ing the recent fall of Constantinople, the route to the Holy Land was firmly in the hands of the Ottomans and there was great potential danger for a small group of western 'unbelievers' making their way to honour the sacred sites in Jerusalem. But the gods smiled on them favourably and they reached the Holy City without further incident on 11 September 1470.

Once there, they stayed in the Franciscan monastery on Mount Zion and visited all the Holy Places they had come so far to see: the ruins of the Temple, the grave of St. Anne, the houses of Herod and Pilate, and, as apotheosis, the Church of the Holy Sepulchre. The monks in the monastery told them how three weeks earlier a group of forty or so pilgrims had succumbed to disease on the road to Jerusalem. The dead included their three former companions, who had left them in Rome. Anselm's bold decision to avoid the Venetian galleys and make a much longer and more difficult journey by an alternative route had probably saved all their lives. Or at least so far because to return to Bruges, the group would now have to pass many of the same places

■ A visit to the Church of the Holy Sepulchre was the culmination of a pilgrimage to the Holy Land. Miniature from *Livre des merveilles* (Book of Miracles). *15th century. Paris, National Library of France, Ms. français 2810, fol. 125.*

as the pilgrims who perished. Anselm and his friends were terrified at the prospect of becoming similarly contaminated, but they had no real choice: it was the only way to get home.

On 22 September, the group set out on their return journey with a heavy heart. At Ramleh, near Jaffa, they had no option but to stay at a pilgrims' inn, where there was a high risk of infection by plague. To make matters worse, they were not allowed to leave for a number of days. The coast was being terrorized by Christian pirates and the local people sought to take out their frustrations on the pilgrims trapped in their city. It was only after two weeks and the personal intervention of a high officer of the sultan that they were finally able to move on.

From Ramleh, they went to Nazareth and the Sea of Galilee, en route for Damascus (14 October) and Beirut (29 October). There they found a Venetian captain who was prepared to take them via Cyprus to Rhodes. But nothing was as it seemed in this twilight zone between the Muslim East and the Christian West. Just as they were boarding the boat, Anselm and his companions were arrested by soldiers of the local emir, who had no doubt been tipped off that these wealthy foreign visitors were worth ransoming. And indeed, it was only after the payment of a huge bail that the emir was willing to let his prisoners go.

Full of joy and happiness, like a hare that has escaped from wild dogs, we boarded our ship, giving praise and thanks to God, St. John the Baptist, St. Catherine and the whole company of saints that we might return safe and well to our own fellow believers, away from the Moors who had never welcomed us as people, but treated us as beasts or animals that have no reason for existence.

On 10 November, they landed at Rhodes and found a Spanish boat to take them to Brindisi, where they arrived on 25 November. After five tension-filled months in the Islamic world, they were now back safe and sound in Christian Europe! From here, the journey continued on horseback. Via Bari and Naples, they made their way to Rome (11 January 1471), where they were greeted by family and friends, who thrilled at the stories about their almost unimaginable adventures. Anselm was again received by the pope and the company took several days to recover their strength and visit the Eternal City once more. By 18 February, they were in Venice, having first passed through the Renaissance splendour of Sienna, Florence, Bologna, Ferrara and Padua. The Doge's city was in the middle of its carnival season and the men from Bruges made their presence felt at several of the balls and dinners organized in the weeks prior to Lent.

On 6 March, they began the long final trek back to Flanders, being feted along the way at Strasburg, Worms, Cologne, Aachen (*where the people are cheerful and the women pretty*) and Antwerp (*the most beautiful city in Brabant*). The news of their imminent arrival went ahead of them,

so that family and friends were waiting to greet them at the city gates when they finally reached Bruges as evening fell on 4 April 1471, after a remarkable and dangerous odyssey of some 14 months. Understandably, the reunion was an emotional one, perhaps in particular for Jan Adornes, who had not seen his mother for six years. He remained in Bruges for the next six months, and during all that time he never clipped the beard he had started to grow when he set off from Pavia for Jerusalem. He also used those six months to write up his account of their amazing adventures along the way.

■ **This magnificent silver resurrection reliquary was commissioned by Anselm or Jan Adornes.**
Adornes collection.

Ꝑ De ingreſſu in templum dñici ſepulcri et proceſſione iniƀi facta
ad loca ſacra·

D Je·rij· Julij ƀora veſperatū in iꝑm venerandū dñici ſepul·
cri templū a paganis id eſt rectoriƀus iꝑius ciuitatis ſancte
Jeroſolime ſuimꝰ admiſſi et numerati·oſtijs ꝑ eos apertis·
pro qua re vnuſquiſꝗ noſtrū quinꝗ eꝛſoluit ducatos·nec
vnꝗ alias ƀoc aperitur templū ab eis·niſi vel propter aduenietes pere·
grinos·velfratres mutandos qui iƀi pro cuſtodia deputātur· Moꝗ
nobis intromiſſis templū clauſerūt· Jntrauerūt aute nobiſcū Gardia·
nus iꝑe et plures ſuoꝛ cõfratrū· Quaprimū aūt deuotus quiſꝗ ꝯpia·
nus vel peregrinꝰ in templū ƀoc pedem poſuerit· plenariā cõſequitur
remiſſionem·

Eſt autē ƀec diſpoſitio templt eius dem ſacratiſſimi· Eccleſia iꝑa rotū·
da eſt·et ƀaƀet ꝑ diametrū inter columnas ſeptuaginta tres pedes··ab·
ſideſꝗ que ƀaƀent ꝑ circuitū a muro exteriori eccleſie dece pedes ſuper
ſepulcrū dñi·qꝭ in mediū eius dem eccleſie eſt apertura rotunda·ita vt
tota cripta ſancti ſepulcri ſit ſuƀ diuo·Galgatƀana autē eccleſia adƀe·
ret iſti·et eſt oblonga loco cƀori eccleſie ſancti ſepulcri adiũcta·ſed parū
demiſſior·ſunt tamē ambe ſuƀ vno tecto·Spelunca in qua eſt ſepulcrū
dñi ƀaƀet in lõgitudine octo pedes·in latitudine ſimiliter octo/vndiꝗ
tecta marmore exteriꝰ·ſed interiꝰ eſt rupes vna ſicut fuit tpe ſepulture

News of Anselm's return was soon on everyone's lips. His prestige in Bruges had been high before his departure, but his successful pilgrimage boosted it to new heights. The names Adornes and Jerusalem were now mentioned in the same breath. Inspired by his journey, Anselm drew up plans to demolish his father's Jerusalem Chapel and replace it with a new house of prayer that was an exact copy of the Church of the Holy Sepulchre in Jerusalem itself - a fitting shrine for the Holy Relics.

■ Detail from the monumental tomb of Anselm Adornes and Margareta van der Banck. Anselm is wearing the chain of the Scottish Order of the Unicorn around his neck.
Jerusalem Chapel.

■ Left. The design of the Jerusalem Chapel was inspired by the Church of the Holy Sepulchre in Jerusalem.
Drawing of the Church of the Holy Sepulchre by Erhard Reuwich, published in Bernhard van Breydenbach, Sanctae Peregrinationes, Mainz, 1486.

Royal adviser and international diplomat

Anselm was now at the pinnacle of his powers. He moved in the very highest circles, was respected by everyone, was fabulously wealthy and was a knight in the Scottish Order of the Unicorn. He was the lord of Cortachy (in Angus, Scotland), Nieuwburg (in Oostkamp), Gentbrugge (in Hertsberge and Ruddervoorde), 's Lands Heeren Walle (in Koekelare) and Ronsele. He also owned property in Moerkerke, Sint-Catharina-buiten-Damme, Oostkerke and Dudzele.

At the start of October 1471, only six months after his return from his pilgrimage, Anselm was once again on his travels, this time with his wife Margareta to Scotland. They were part of the group accompanying Mary Stuart and Thomas and Robert Boyd, who after two years of foreign exile were being allowed to return to Edinburgh. Anselm presented King James III with a copy of his pilgrimage account, with a dedication that he hoped would help the king *to win an incontestable victory* over his adversaries. Anselm's ties with Scotland continued to strengthen. He was appointed as custodian of the Scottish privileges throughout the Burgundian Empire and was awarded the income from estates in Forfar and Perthshire.

The knowledge he acquired during his pilgrimage and his meetings with the pope

■ **At the request of the Burgundian duke Charles the Bold, Anselm Adornes embarked on a journey to Persia to negotiate an alliance against the Turks.**
Workshop of Rogier van der Weyden, Portrait of Charles the Bold. *1460. Berlijn, Gemäldegalerie, inv. 545.*

and other leaders, both religious and secular, also brought him to the attention of Duke Charles the Bold. Like his father before him, Charles was a fanatic in the Christian battle against 'the infidel', driven on by a desire for military glory and a mystical yearning to serve what he saw as a higher calling in the name of God and Christendom.

It seemed to him that Anselm was the ideal person to help prepare a coalition against the Turks. With this in mind, he sent Anselm, together with the Franciscan monk Lodovico Severi, on a diplomatic mission to Persia. The purpose was to persuade Shah Uzun Hassan to enter into an

■ This priceless painting was on board a ship seized by Polish pirates. During his visit to Danzig, Anselm Adornes unsuccessfully attempted to secure the release of both the ship and the painting.
Hans Memling, The Last Judgement. *1467-71.*
© *Muzeum Narodowe, Gdansk, Poland.*

CASIMIRUS der Kö:
nig Zn polen König h LUDWIH:
Jn Vngern Sohn Jst gebo: 1446
desto: 1492

ELISABETH Sin
Semablin Keiser AELBRECHT
z Tochter Jst geba: gesto

alliance against the Ottoman Empire. For the second time in just a few years, Anselm set off on a long and perilous journey through strange and unknown lands. They travelled via the Baltic and Eastern Europe. At the end of April 1474, the mission was received at the court of the Polish king Casimir IV. Anselm took the opportunity to raise the matter of the return of the 'San Matteo', a galley chartered by his friend Tommaso Portinari which had been seized in Danzig the previous year, along with its precious cargo, including the painting of *The Last Judgement* by Hans Memling. This time, the Adornes powers of persuasion failed him and the ship and its contents remained in Polish hands. In fact, the painting can still be seen in the National Museum in Danzig.

Following this rare failure, Anselm suddenly and unexpectedly returned to Bruges. The reason for this has never been clear, but we do know that Fra Lodovico continued with the mission alone, although he was unsuccessful in raising support for a new crusade.

A fallen giant

On 5 January 1477, the army of Charles the Bold suffered a crushing defeat at the Battle of Nancy. The duke himself was among the many dead. Rule over the Burgundian Empire now passed into the hands of his

■ In April 1474, during a diplomatic mission on behalf of Charles the Bold, Anselm Adornes was received at the court of King Casimir IV of Poland.
Anonymous, Portrait of Casimir IV, King of Poland, and his wife. *16th century.* © Muzeum Narodowe, Gdansk, Poland.

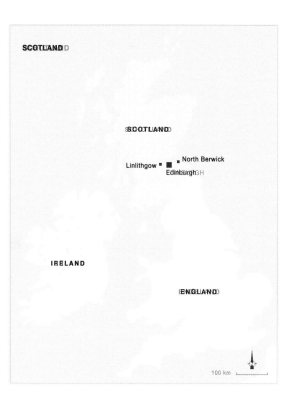

SCOTLAND

SCOTLAND

Linlithgow ■ ■ ■ North Berwick
Edinburgh

IRELAND

ENGLAND

100 km

only daughter, Mary of Burgundy. Many of the cities that had been harshly treated during Charles' reign saw this as an opportunity to rise in rebellion to seek redress for past grievances. Bruges was one such city. Duchess Mary asked Louis of Gruuthuse, Anselm Adornes and a number of the city's other leading patricians to try and negotiate a compromise solution. Initially, some progress seemed to be made and the uproar died down, only to burst out again with renewed vigour at the end of March. This time no compromise was possible. Anselm and several other patricians were arrested and accused of enriching themselves unfairly at the expense of the people. Some judicious bribery and corruption quickly secured their release, but not for long. They were picked up again at the start of May and subjected to the full rigour of the law. Anselm Adornes, the once highly respected patrician, was tortured on the rack to force him into confessing his 'crimes'. Other forms of humiliation were also heaped upon him. He was made to beg publically for mercy, bare-headed and dressed only in an *unbelted black tabard*. He was barred from holding further public office in the city and was condemned to pay four times over the money he had gained from his 'dishonest practices'. He was further obliged to pay 250 pounds of silver groats into the city treasury - a significant sum equivalent to four years' salary for a master mason.

This effectively put an end to his political career in Bruges, although he retained the confidence of the duchess and was able to hold his position of guardian of the Lepers' House.

■ **The Scottish king James III made Anselm Adornes a Knight in the Order of the Unicorn. This replica of the order's chain was made on the basis of the images depicted in the Jerusalem Chapel.**
Adornes collection.

From now, his attention was focused increasingly on Scotland, sometimes at the request of Mary of Burgundy. His relations with James III remained intact and the king appointed him as captain of the royal palace at Linlithgow. He acquired three houses in the most prestigious street in the town and took up residence in a fine mansion in Blackness, where, amongst others, he received and entertained the king. However, he soon found himself being increasingly drawn into the conspiracies and intrigues that were rife in the Scottish court. As a foreigner and a personal friend of James, he was a perfect target for the king's enemies. After a bloody coup in 1482, during which several of the king's supporters were killed, Anselm knew that it was only a matter of time before he would be next. He drew up a will in which he defiantly declared that nothing would prevent him from serving the king and that he was prepared to die if need be, just as the Lord Jesus had died for the salvation of mankind. He asked for a number of practical arrangements to be made for his burial and the notification of his family in Flanders. He then left all his properties in Scotland to Efemie, his illegitimate Scottish daughter.

Although he knew the risk he was running, Anselm agreed to act as an intermediary with the king's rebellious brother. But before he undertook this dangerous task, he wanted to prepare himself by making a pilgrimage in honour of Our Lady, whose protection during his forthcoming mission he wished to seek. On 23 January 1483, he walked to a convent at North Berwick. After the evening meal, at around eight o'clock, a force of 18 knights and 200 foot soldiers surrounded the building. Anselm's manservant was forced to tell the intruders where his master could be found. But instead of seeking to hide or run away, Anselm walked bravely up to the men he knew had come to kill him. All that he asked was that the sisters in the convent be spared, following which he was felled by three massive sword blows, one that tore open his chest from shoulder to heart, one that gashed his leg and a third that split his skull. His murderers then robbed him of his knight's chain, his jewels and his clothes, before disappearing into the night.

The nuns washed and embalmed his body. After a short service in the convent chapel, he was carried on a bier to St. Michael's Church in Linlithgow, where he was buried in accordance with his own instructions. When news of his death reached Bruges, it was not only the bells of the Jerusalem Chapel that tolled in mourning, but also the bells of the churches of Our Lady, St. Donatian and St. Walburga. On 3 March 1483, a funeral service was held in his honour in the family chapel, well attended by many of the city's leading dignitaries. Later, his heart was returned to Bruges in a lead casket and buried in a monumental tomb in the chapel, alongside *his beloved companion* Margareta, who had been laid to rest there in 1480.

■ These lead badges were found in the casket
containing the heart of Anselm Adornes.
Adornes collection.

■ View of the almshouses.

FROM ADORNES TO
DE LIMBURG STIRUM

1429

The brothers **Pieter II and Jacob Adornes erect a chapel dedicated to the Passion of Christ and the Holy Sepulchre on the corner of the Peperstraat and the Balstraat.** Archive documents show that the chapel was still not completed by 1439. The Adornes go in search for the additional resources necessary to finish the work.

The residence of Pieter II is next to the chapel.

1454

Carthusian monks are appointed as 'guardians' of the Jerusalem Foundation. Until the end of the 18th century, they continue to jointly sign all accounts and invoices.

1469

Anselm Adornes († 1483) is nominated by the family as their sole administrator for the Jerusalem Foundation. The residence of Pieter II is also transferred to Anselm.

1471-83

After his pilgrimage, Anselm Adornes demolishes the existing chapel. He builds a new and larger Jerusalem Chapel. The work is completed before his death in 1483.

During this period Anselm also builds six almshouses to accommodate twelve poor and needy women. There are two rooms to each house, one downstairs and one upstairs. Each room has its own fireplace.

Anselm also renovates the dilapidated residence and transforms it into a fine patrician mansion. The mansion is connected to the main chapel by a passageway above an arcade. At the end of the narrow passage there is a small private prayer chapel.

1483-90

The administration of the Jerusalem Foundation passes into the hands of Anselm's oldest son, Jan Adornes († 1511), canon of the St. Peter's Church in Lille. He makes arrangements for the interior fittings (floors, stairs, doors to the upper

■ **The monumental tomb.** *Jerusalem Chapel.*

■ **Right. Jan Adornes, son of Anselm, commissioned this reliquary to hold the relic of the Holy Cross.** *Adornes collection, Jerusalem Chapel.*

chapel, etc.) and luxurious embellishment (altar cloths, curtains, cushions, candlesticks, monstrances, etc.) of the chapel. The monumental tomb of Anselm and Margareta, sculpted by master-mason Cornelis Tielman, is installed. A Calvary is erected in front of the chancel and against the wall of the crypt.

1493

The earliest mention of the presence of the relic of the Holy Cross in the Jerusalem Chapel.

■ **From the 15th century onwards, the Jerusalem Chapel, with the golden ball on its tower, was an unmistakeable part of the Bruges skyline.**
Detail from the St. Nicholas Retable. *Last quarter of the 15th century. Bruges, Groeninge Museum. © www.lukasweb. be - Art in Flanders vzw foto Hugo Maertens, Dominique Provost.*

1511

Jan is succeeded as administrator of the Jerusalem Foundation by his younger brother Arnoud Adornes († 1517), who was ordained as a priest following the death of his wife. He has been living in the mansion next to the chapel since 1482.

1512

Arnoud is the last male descendant of Anselm. His only child is a daughter, Agnes, who is married to Andreas de la Coste. Arnoud therefore decides to transfer the name, coat of arms and all privileges of the Adornes family to his grandson, Jan de la Coste, who from that moment on goes through life as Jan Adornes.

The square in front of the chapel is paved with cobblestones.

1513-14

The interior portal in oak is installed. The oak furnishings in the sacristy also date from this time.

De la Coste genaamd Adornes

1517

Jan de la Coste, named Adornes, Lord of Nieuwenhove and Nieuwvliet, succeeds his grandfather as administrator of the Jerusalem Foundation.

1523-24

A small annex to the chapel is built by master-mason Cornelis vander Stichele to house an imitation of the Holy Sepulchre. A grave is also made for the Jerusalem pilgrims, probably at the initiative of the Jerusalem Brotherhood, which is affiliated to the chapel.

1530-45

Jan de la Coste, named Adornes, donates a Calvary triptych to the chapel. He († 1537) and his wife Catharina Mettenye († 1545) are buried in the chapel next to the monumental tomb of Anselm.

1560

The stained glass windows with images of the administrators of the Jerusalem Foundation and their wives are installed.

1584-1609

The monastery of the Carthusians is destroyed. They take up residence in the Adornes domain.

■ Jan de la Coste, named Adornes († 1537) commissioned this triptych. In the middle, we can see the crucified Christ with the Blessed Virgin and St. John the Baptist. The side panels portray Jan, his wife and their children.
Adornes collection, Jerusalem Chapel.

1610

Anselm Opitius Adornes, Lord of Nieuwenhove and burgomaster of Bruges, is buried in the Jerusalem Chapel.

1682-95

The six almshouses, which have fallen into disrepair, are renovated. Repair work is also carried out to the chapel and its tower. The court of honour in front of the chapel is repaved.

De Draeck

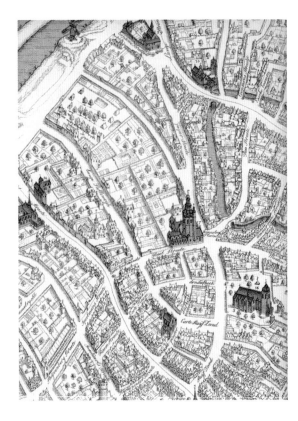

1752-54

Antoon Augustijn Adornes († 1752), married to his second cousin, Marie Françoise de Draeck († 1742), is the last male descendant of Jan de la Coste, named Adornes. His sister, Jacoba Dorothea Adornes († 1754), succeeds him as administrator of the Adornesdomain. After her death, the domain passes into the hands of the de Draeck family.

1772

Three new window frames are installed on the street side of the old family residence to allow in more light.

■ **The Jerusalem Chapel and the Adornes domain. Detail from the map by Marcus Gerards, 1561.**
Adornes collection.

1799

Gaspard Bernard de Draeck protests against the planned demolition of the Jerusalem Chapel by the French administration. He argues that it is a private chapel that can easily be converted into a residence and that the tower is actually a belvedere.

1835

The Apostoline Sisters take up residence in the domain and erect a number of subsidiary buildings, including a house that replaces the wall on the Peperstraat side of the property. The sisters establish a *spellewerckscole* in this house, where young girls and women can learn how to make lace.

1861

The owners protest against the many changes that are being made without their knowledge and only serve the needs of the sisters. Plaster ceilings cover the old vault beams, fireplaces are removed, walls are breached, new doors are installed, old windows bricked up, altered or replaced, simply to facilitate better circulation through the building for the nuns, who now regard it as a convent.

■ Pupils diligently at work in the Lace School (1910). At the back, one of the nuns is keeping a close eye on her class.
Beeldbank Brugge, FO/A09188. 'verz. J. A. Rau'.

■ The Apostoline Sisters giving a lesson in the courtyard (circa 1935). The pupils are wearing white aprons. One girl is spinning thread, another has a lace cushion under her arm and a third is making lace with bobbins.
Beeldbank Brugge, BRU001005364 - G/C746/2.

■ Top. A group of women leaving the chapel. They are dressed in typical Bruges hooded cloaks. They have a white bonnet and are wearing clogs. This photograph dates from circa 1920.
Beeldbank Brugge, FO/A01311 'verz. J. A. Rau'.

■ Below. During the First World War, mattresses were protecting the stained glass windows, as can be seen in this photograph from 1918.
Beeldbank Brugge, FO_C3259.

■ Page 85. This 1925 photograph of the court of honour shows the bricked-up arches under the alleyway and the gate leading to the almshouses.
Brugge, Beeldbank, FO/A01309 en FO/A01310. 'verz. J. A. Rau'.

Bruges
Chapel of Jerusalem 1427
Courtyard.

De Limburg Stirum

1882

Baroness Astérie Albertine de Draeck (1804-1882), married to Count François Joseph de Thiennes (1777-1855), is the last name-bearing descendant of her family. Through her daughter, Marie Thérèse de Thiennes (1828-1909), married to Count Thierry de Limburg Stirum (1827-1911), the domain passes into the hands of their son, Henri de Limburg Stirum (1864-1935).

Ca. 1900

The plasterwork in the chapel is removed to expose the wooden ceiling and brick walls. The polychrome is removed from the altar with the Golgotha crosses and the sandstone balustrade. The organ is thoroughly renovated.

1953

The Jerusalem Chapel is classified as a protected monument.

■ Above right. Baroness Astérie de Draeck, wife of Count François de Thiennes.

■ Above right and under. In 1965 the globe was removed from the tower. Curieus neighbours came to watch the spectacle. These pictures give us a good impression of the globe's size.

■ An aerial photograph of the Adornes domain (ca. 1950).

1965

The chapel is in a poor state of repair. As a precaution, the copper globe of the tower is removed.

The almshouses are abandoned.

1968-72

The chapel and its tower are restored.

1976

The almshouses are also classified as a protected monument.

1986

The sisters leave the domain.

1987

The almshouses, the chapel and part of the domain are leased to the Lace Centre. The almshouses are restored and turned into a lace museum. The Jerusalem Chapel is opened to the public.

2000

Count and Countess Maximilien and Véronique de Limburg Stirum become the current patrons of the Jerusalem Foundation and administrators of the domain. Their motto is 'Sharing to bring alive - bringing alive to preserve'.

2007

The de Limburg Stirum family takes over the management of the domain.

2010

Start of renovation and re-designation work. The 19th century alterations are reversed and the domain is restored to its former glory.

■ Count Henry de Limburg Stirum.

2014

The Lace Centre and the Lace Museum move to the old lace school within the domain. The Adornes domain opens its doors to the public.

■ View of the Lace Centre from the garden.

The Adornes domain in the 21st century

The maintenance of historic buildings is costly. For this reason, many families have found it necessary to relinquish the properties they inherited. The de Limburg Stirum family has chosen to follow a different path, difficult though it might be. As the direct descendants of the founders, they attach great importance to the preservation of the Adornes domain, irrespective of the difficulties. So what is the future for these old stones? This is a question that the family has thought about long and hard. The care and maintenance of our common heritage is not something that can be taken lightly. The Adornesdomain is more than just bricks alone. It is a piece of family history and represents the collective efforts of many different generations. It embodies five centuries of living and thought.

The challenges are many. Merely maintaining the domain in its present condition demands major resources, great commitment and detailed specialist knowledge. But it goes much further than that. The family is concerned to preserve all aspects of the domain's history, not just the immoveable (buildings) and moveable (objects, archives) elements, but also the intangible elements (stories, rituals, usages and traditions). They regard this family heritage as an indivisible whole and are willing make the necessary efforts to allow it to be con-

■ Count and Countess Maximilien and Véronique de Limburg Stirum are the current patrons of the Jerusalem Foundation and administrators of the domain.

■ Right. View from the garden.

served, studied and made available to the public. Since 2010 considerable restoration work has been carried out and in 2014 the domain opened its doors for the first time to public visitors. For the coming years plans are in hand for the construction of the garden. The family also hopes to exhibit a number of historical artefacts and manuscripts, as well as carrying out further renovation.

The Adornes domain is a place that breathes history. Men and women have been living and working here for the past 500 years. During those five centuries countless pilgrims and believers have visited the chapel to pray or celebrate mass. But time does not stand still. Consequently, the family has also decided to make the domain acces-sible for contemporary artists and various socio-cultural projects. The domain is not just a museum. It is a remarkable cocktail of ancient structures, precious objects, fascinating stories and modern creations, all served with a strong dash of family tradition.

Maximilien and Véronique de Limburg Stirum have transformed the Adornes domain into a historical crossroads where yesterday, today and tomorrow all meet. They have given a house steeped in history a new soul, with respect for the past and an eye to the future.

There is nothing like a dream for creating the future. (Victor Hugo)

THE JERUSALEM CHAPEL and the ADORNESDOMEIN from A to Z

Almshouses – During the 15th century a number of poor beguines lived on the Adornes domain in the 'Ten Hamerkine' convent. The last of these beguines died around 1455. In his will, Anselm Adornes gave instructions for the construction of *twelve brick rooms, each with its own fireplace, where twelve needy widows might live.* Six so-called almshouses were built on the Balstraat side of the domain, each housing two women in an upstairs and a downstairs room. The women were given a monthly pension and received wood or turf for burning on the Feast of St. Martin. On other feast days they were sometimes given bread and wine, or even money. They were required to follow a strict regime. Amongst other things, they were obliged to attend daily evening prayers in the chapel, were expected to always sleep in their own beds and put their lights out by a certain time, and were not allowed male visitors. The first house closest to the chapel was home to the vergeress. She was responsible for cleaning the chapel, polishing the copper and washing the linen, as well as buying bread and wine for the mass and coal for heating. During religious services she carried the collection dish amongst the congregation, with the proceeds being divided between the twelve women.

Balustrade – Behind the Calvary there is a balustrade or choir screen in white stone. The lower part is original. It dates from the 15th century and displays the familiar Adornes attributes: the family coat of arms, the sunburst clouds, St. Catherine's wheel, the Jerusalem cross and the chain of the Order of the Unicorn.

■ View of the Calvary and the upper chapel, in front of which stands the monumental tomb of Anselm Adornes and his wife.

GROUND PLAN OF THE ADORNES DOMAIN

- ☐ The Jerusalem Chapel
- ☐ The almshouses
- ☐ The Adornes mansion
- ☐ Later additions
- ▨ Court of honour

10 m

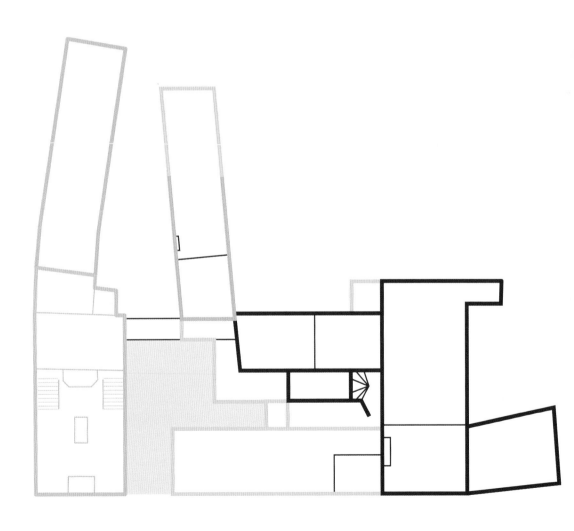

Brotherhood of Jerusalem – The Brotherhood of Jerusalem was already associated with the chapel as early as the late 15th century. Their activities were focused mainly on Palm Sunday and the Feast of the Elevation of the Holy Cross (14 September). Members of the brotherhood were allowed to be buried in the chapel crypt, the capstone of which was placed in 1523 and is still visible. The brotherhood cut its ties with the chapel in the 16th century as a result of a dispute with Jan Adornes († 1537).

Byzantine cross *(not on display)* – This palm wood cross is decorated with miniature carved scenes from the life of Christ and the Virgin Mary. It was probably brought back by Anselm and Jan from their pilgrimage to the Holy Land. The silver embellishment was added later: the crucified Christ and the sunburst clouds emblem. It is kept in a leather custode, which also bears the same clouds emblem.

Calvary – A monumental Latin cross flanked by two Tau crosses tower above a white sandstone Calvary, in which the Instruments of the Passion are sculpted: the column, the purse with Judas's 20 pieces of silver, the lantern, the rod, the whip, the lance of Longinus, two ladders, the ruined tower, the hammer, the tongs, the nails, the

■ Between the coat of arms of Anselm Adornes (left) and the impaled escutcheon of the Adornes and Van der Banck families (right), it is possible to read the heraldic device Para tutum, meaning 'Prepare for us a safe way'.

rope, the stick with the sponge, the bucket filled with vinegar, Christ's garments and the dice used to cast lots for them. Together with the skulls and the bones they visualize in a poignant manner the suffering of Christ. At the top, there is an angel wearing a crown of thorns. The totality symbolizes Golgotha, the hill where Christ was crucified, and it serves as an altar piece. The alcoves with doors in copper lattice work are for keeping relics. The spaces between the doors are decorated with carved scenes from the Passion, surmounted by family coats of arms.

Chandelier – Above the monumental tomb of Anselm and Margareta hangs a decorative 16th century Renaissance brass chandelier, which must have been a very costly item in its day. This multi-armed candelabra is highly decorative and exudes wealth. It is crowned by a 'wild man' figure holding a drawn sword. On the underside there is double-headed lion is biting in a ring formed by two dolphins.

Clock – Against the front gable of the chapel, high above the entrance portal, there once hung a clock. Probably installed in the early 16th century, it can be seen in the 1641 drawing of the chapel by Antonius Sanderus.

Clouds – Clouds illuminated by the rays of the sun or sunburst clouds were used as a symbol for the Adornes family. The emblem can be found at numerous places in the chapel and the adjacent mansion, and has also now been adopted as the logo for the Adornes domain.

Coats of arms – Numerous coats of arms can be seen all over the chapel. They are an expression of the self-confidence of the patrician class as a whole, but also underline the personal nature of the chapel.

Colour – Try to imagine what the chapel must have looked like around 1500. All the walls were plastered and painted. The

■ The family were able to follow religious services in the upper chapel from their private prayer chapel.

altars cloths would have been bright red and the curtains crimson and green, with others in blue. The chairs and pews would have been covered with richly embroidered cushions bearing the family coat of arms and emblems. The Calvary and its crosses would also have been brightly painted, as would the wooden panelling around the monumental tomb. In short, a riot of colour.

Court of Honour – The Court of Honour is reached through the large gate on the Peperstraat. This was the domain's central courtyard. The 19th century wing on the right now houses the reception and the museum shop. Opposite the entrance gate is the passage leading to the almshouses. On the left, a small door gives access to the chapel.

Cross of St. Andrew – The X-shaped cross of St. Andrew refers both to Anselm's connection with Scotland (where Andrew is the patron saint) and to the dukes of Burgundy (whose guardian saint he was). The lower panels of the doors in the chapel that give access to the upper chapel are decorated with embossed St. Andrew crosses. The same motif can also be found in the parapet of the gallery at the top of the tower.

Crypt – The entrances to the crypt are under the staircases leading to the upper chapel. The crypt has its own altar. The consoles of the cross-rib vaulting bear the polychromed coats of arms of Anselm and Margareta. The capstone in the floor seals the tomb in which members of the Brotherhood of Jerusalem were buried.

Device – In heraldry, a device is a motto. Anselm Adornes' device was *Para tutum*, meaning 'prepare for us a safe way', a text taken from the Marian hymn *Ave maris stella*. His oldest son Jan took *Tandem* ('At last') as his device. It can be seen on his commemorative monument above the entrance door and on the reliquary cross in the crypt.

Epitaphs – The exuberant Baroque epitaph or commemorative monument on the west wall of the chapel attracts the attention of every visitor. The central carving shows the Crucifixion, with the Blessed Virgin, St. John and Mary Magdalen. To the left kneels Anselmus Opitius Adornes († 1610), to the right his wife, Anna van Braecle († 1636). Both are richly dressed and wear a millstone ruff around their neck. The sunburst clouds at the bottom of the side panels are a typical emblem of the Adornes family. This elaborate monument in marble and alabaster contrasts starkly with the more sober monument to Jeroom Adornes († 1558), which is situated on the other side of the chapel, near the pulpit. He is depicted in full armour, kneeling in front of a prayer stool, with his helmet and gauntlets on the ground. Traces of polychrome can still be seen and the Adornes coat of arms and cloud emblem are also prominently visible. His motto on the banderole reads *Non force* (not with violence).

■ Mass celebrated in the Jerusalem Chapel for the de Limburg Stirum family, September 2015.

■ Left. The Instruments of the Passion, sculpted in white sandstone, are intended to visualize Christ's suffering and death.

Funerary hatchments – The wall in the upper chapel is hung with a number of black, diamond-shaped boards. These are funerary hatchments, which display the coat of arms and date of death of a deceased person. Sometimes known as an *obiit* (the Latin word for 'died'), they were originally displayed in the house where the deceased passed away, before later being transferred to the chapel where he was buried. The most recent funerary hatchment in the Jerusalem Chapel dates from 1998 and shows the impaled escutcheon of the de Limburg Stirum and de Ligne families.

■ This postcard shows the condition of the Holy Sepulchre Chapel in 1921. Note the absence of the lattice work and the white altar cloth.
Beeldbank Brugge, FO/A01333 'verz. J. A. Rau'.

■ Page 101. The Madonna Enthroned triptych is one of the finest works in the chapel.

Grave plates – Alongside the staircase leading to the organ loft hang fragments of the copper grave plate that originally covered the grave of Jan Adornes († 1537) and his wife Catharina Metteneye († 1545), who were buried next to the monumental tomb of Anselm and Margareta.

Impaled escutcheon – An impaled escutcheon is a shield that bears the combined coats of arms of two families joined by marriage. Coats of arms of this kind can be seen at various points in the chapel, with the arms of Anselm Adornes' family on the left and the arms of Margareta vander Banck's family on the right. The Calvary bears the impaled escutcheons of the Adornes–Bailleul (mid 16th century) and Adornes–van Braecle (late 16th cen-

tury) families. In Pieter II's mansion there is a similar combined coat of arms for the Adornes–Braderic families.

Jerusalem cross – The Jerusalem cross is a large 'cross potent' or crutch cross, with four smaller Greek crosses, one in each quadrant. This 'five-fold' cross represents the five wounds of Christ. It was the symbol of the Kingdom and the City of Jerusalem and was also used by the Knights of the Holy Sepulchre. It can be seen on the balustrade behind the Calvary and on the capstone sealing the grave of the Jerusalem pilgrims in the crypt.

Lead badges – While investigating the burial chambers of the monumental tomb, archaeologists discovered the lead casket

in which Anselm's heart was brought back to Bruges from Scotland. Inside, they also found three lead badges with the letters 'JHRM' (for Jerusalem) on one side and a sunburst cloud, the emblem of the Adornes family, on the other side.

Monumental tomb – In front of the Calvary and its altar stands the monumental black tomb bearing the images of Anselm Adornes and Margareta vander Banck. He is dressed in full armour, with his feet resting on a lion, the symbol of courage and strength. She wears a richly draped dress and a fashionable hennin on her head, with a dog at her feet to symbolize faithfulness. They lie side by side, praying through all eternity to the images of Christ's Passion. Between them rests Anselm's shield and

helmet. Margareta is actually buried here, but Anselm's last resting place is Linlithgow in Scotland. Only his heart was brought back to Bruges for interment in the tomb.

Organ – Above the entrance portal there is an organ dating from 1760, probably made by the Bruges organ-builder Andries Jacob Berger. It underwent major remodelling around 1900, but several of the original pipes were preserved.

Passageway *(not accessible)* – The upper floor of Pieter II's mansion was connected to the upper chapel by a passageway. In the corner to the right of the altar it is possible to see the small door that gave access to this passageway.

Portal – The oak entrance portal was sculpted in 1513-14 by master-carpenter Hendrik Sceewale. The panels are decorated with typical Gothic scrollwork. The locks, mountings and hinges are original.

Prayer chapel *(not accessible)* – Alongside the upper chapel there is a small private prayer chapel, reached via the passageway from the adjoining mansion. This painted octagonal chamber allowed the family to follow the liturgical services performed in the upper chapel through small windows. Note also the diagonal viewing slit that offered a view of the lower altar in front of the Calvary.

■ Anselm Adornes. Detail of the stained glass window.

■ Left. The richly decorated epitaph monument to Anselmus Opitius Adornes (✝ 1610) and his wife Anna van Braecle (✝ 1636) adorns the west wall of the chapel.

Pulpit – The pulpit dates from the 17th century. Its decoration reflects the veneration of the Holy Cross and the Passion of Christ. St. Helen holds Christ's cross. Angels carry the whipping column and the lance of Longinus. Also depicted are the Veil of Veronica, Christ's robes, the cockerel (that crowed three times when Peter denied his master), the jar and bowl in which Pilate washed his hands in innocence, and the Crown of Thorns.

Reliquary cross – This reliquary in silver gilt was made around 1500 to hold the relic of the Holy Cross. The motto *Tandem* ('At last') shows that the cross was commissioned by Jan Adornes (✝ 1511), Anselm's eldest son. It is kept in an alcove in the crypt behind an openwork wrought-iron door dating from 1713.

Resurrection reliquary *(not on display)* – The triumphant risen Christ steps with his right leg out of the tomb. In his left hand he holds the victory pennant, while his right is raised in a sign of blessing. Two angels hold open the cover of his grave. Lower down, relics from the Holy Sepulchre are displayed behind a pane of glass. This reliquary was commissioned by Anselm or Jan Adornes and displays silverwork of the very highest quality. Bruges, late 15th-early 16th century.

Sacristy *(not accessible)* – A rectangular door in the north wall of the crypt on the Balstraat side leads to the sacristy. The room is lit by two barred windows and has an exit towards the almshouse quarter of the domain. The oak furnishings date from the early 16th century.

Sepulchre of Christ – A low opening at the back of the crypt leads into the Chapel of the Holy Sepulchre, an imitation of the actual Holy Sepulchre in Jerusalem. At the foot of the altar, a wrought-iron screen protects the sepulchre and the recumbent figure of Christ (which used to be carried through the city during religious processions). An extractor has been installed above the candelabrum.

Stained glass windows – Six pointed arches provide the chapel with light, two in each side gable and two in the front gable. Each contains stained glass windows dating from 1560, depicting important members of the Adornes family with their patron saints and their coats of arms. The figures in the side gables are looking towards the altar; the figures in the front gable are looking at each other. These are rare examples of 16th century glass art that have survived intact in their original location.

- Pieter I Adornes (with St. Peter) and Elisabeth van de Walle (with St. Elisabeth of Hungary).
- Pieter II Adornes (with St. Peter) and Elisabeth Braderic (with St. Elisabeth of Hungary). Pieter II was the founder of the first Jerusalem Chapel.
- Anselm Adornes (with St. Anselm, Archbishop of Canterbury) and Margareta vander Banck (with St. Margaret and the dragon, her traditional attribute). Anselm was the founder of the second (current) Jerusalem Chapel. Note his motto *Para tutum* and the chain of the Order of the Unicorn around his neck.
- Arnoud Adornes (with St. Arnold, depicted as a knight wearing a cope on top of his armour) and Agnes van Nieuwenhove (with St. Agnes and her lamb). Arnoud was the son of Anselm and patron of the Jerusalem Foundation.
- Jan de la Coste, named Adornes (with St. John the Baptist) and Catharina Metteneye (with St. Catherine of Alexandria). Jan was also patron of the Jerusalem Foundation.
- The brothers Jeroom Adornes (with St. Jerome, cardinal and church elder)

and Jacob Adornes (with the apostle St. James the Lesser), sons of Jan de la Coste, named Adornes.

- **Statues** – Above both the doors that lead to the upper chapel there are statues of the Virgin Mary and St. John standing on corbels. It was probably the initial intention to place statues of Anselm and Margareta here. The design plans for these statues still exist in the domain's archives. It is not clear why the plans were never carried out, although this may have something to do with Anselm's difficult position after the Bruges troubles of 1477.

Sun – See 'tower'.

Sword – The traditional attribute of St. Catherine. See 'wheel'.

Tabernacle – The tabernacle or sacrament tower is made from white stone and marble, and dates from the late 16th-early 17th century. The burning oil lamps placed at each of the four corners symbolize watchfulness. The pelican at the top refers to the Eucharist. At the bottom we can see the Adornes coat of arms.

Tower – When approaching the Jerusalem Chapel, it is the tall, octagonal tower that first catches the attention. High pointed arch windows and an openwork gallery give the brick structure a lighter aspect. This is surmounted by an ochre-coloured wooden construction, crowned by a copper globe,

■ This commemorative plaque for Jan Adornes, son of Anselm, displays all the family's traditional attributes. At the top, the Cross of Jerusalem, the family coat of arms and St. Catherine's wheel. At the bottom, the sunburst clouds. Jan's motto Tandem (At last!) can be seen above the skull.

which in medieval times was covered with gold leaf (as can be seen on the Retable of St. Nicholas by the Master of the Legend of St. Lucy in the Groeninge Museum). Right at the very top there is an iron cross with a broken wheel and a palm branch. The broken wheel represents St. Catherine and Anselm's journey to her grave on Mount Sinai, while the palm leaf stands for his visit to Jerusalem. The slender corner towers are decorated with a gilt sickle moon (the symbol for the Virgin Mary and the Church, as well as Islam and the Orient) and a radiant sun (the symbol for God). The Cross of St. Andrew in the balustrade refers both to the Dukes of Burgundy and to Scotland.

Triptych – Madonna Enthroned with Child, flanked by music-making angels. The Virgin Mary wears an impressive broad red cloak, trimmed with gold brocade and semi-precious stones. On her lap sits the Infant Jesus, dressed in a white shirt and looking at a breviary. On the left, St. Catherine is also reading, while holding a sword in her other hand. Her wheel can be seen in the bottom left-hand corner. St. Barbara stands on the right, likewise leafing through a book. Behind her we can see the tower, her traditional attribute. The left corner also contains a peacock feather, symbol for the immortality of the soul. Bruges, early 16th century.

Triptych – Christ on the Cross, with the Blessed Virgin and the Apostle John. On the left stands Jan de la Coste, named Adornes († 1537), accompanied by his patron saint,

John the Baptist (with the lamb), and his seven sons, the oldest of whom, Jeroom, looks directly at the viewer. Pierken, who only lived for a day, is also depicted as a young boy. On the right stands Catharina Metteneye († 1545), with her patron saint, St. Catherine (with the sword), and her four daughters, two of whom are nuns. Her wide cape is embroidered with the Metteneye family coat of arms. In the background we can see the towers of Bruges, including the silhouette of the Jerusalem Chapel in the right panel.

Unicorn – the chain of the Scottish Order of the Unicorn can be seen in the beam bolsters, the balustrade behind the Calvary and the stained glass window in which Anselm is depicted.

Upper chapel – Two staircases, each of 14 steps, lead up on the left and right to the upper chapel. The wooden cross-rib vaulting of the tower is clearly visible. The altar is dedicated to St. Catherine and contains numerous relics. On the wall alongside the altar there are memorial tablets in marble and alabaster to Jacob IV Adornes († 1572) and his two wives, Livina van der Zype and Françoise van Belle. On the right there is a similar tablet commemorating Jacob V Adornes († 1662). Coat of arms decorate the stained glass windows and the consoles.

Wheel – The wheel is the attribute of St. Catherine, who was a very popular saint in medieval Flanders. Catherine lived in Alexandria (Egypt) and was very devout.

When the Emperor Maxentius sent forty wise men to persuade her to recant her
Christian faith, she instead succeeded in
converting them to Christianity. Frustrated,
the angry emperor tried to have her broken
on the wheel, but the wheel broke and not
Catherine. He then ordered her to be be-
headed by sword, the other attribute with
which she is often depicted.

■ The wooden cross-rib vaulting of the tower.

Walk: In the footsteps of the Adornes

1/ Jeruzalemstraat 39. The 16th century gable of this house was 'artfully restored' in 1916, including an added reference to the neighbouring Adornesdomain. Can you find the family coat of arms? And can you see the Jerusalem cross?

2/ Verversdijk. The place where the 'Europa College' now stands was once the site of the residential complex of Anselm Adornes, with its inn, dyeing shops, warehouses and stables. Just opposite was the Schottendijk (Scots' Dyke), now the Sint-Annarei.

3/ Spinolarei 9. It was at this spot that Pieter I Adornes lived in a house named 'Het Groot Galjoen' (The Great Galleon).

4/ Jan van Eyckplein 6. The 'Witte Poorte'(White Gate) House was property of Pieter I Adornes and his descendants. Walk through the courtyard to the back of the house. In the corner on the right you can still see the coat of arms of Margareta vander Banck, the wife of Anselm. A few houses further you can find the Toll House, with the *Pijndershuis* (Porters' House) alongside.

5/ Burghers' Lodge. It was in this building, the meeting place of the Bruges burghers, that the *Witte Beer* (White Bear) jousting fraternity had its headquarters, as can be seen from the bear in the gable.

6/ The old Beursplein, site of the nation house of the Genoese merchants (now the Frietmuseum) and the former inn of the Van der Beurse family.

■ Left. The wall of the Burgher's Lodge is graced with a statue of the Bruges bear. This is a reference to the *Witte Beer* (White Bear) jousting club that used to meet here.

■ Right. The old Beursplein (Beurs Square) got its name from the house of the Van der Beurse family. The former nation house of the Genoese merchants is on the left.

7/ Kraanplein. This is where the city crane once stood and incoming ships were unloaded. The Kraanrei canal, which ran from the Burghers' Lodge to the Water Hall on the Market Square, has now been vaulted over.

8/ Vlamingstraat 17. This is where the 'Ter Baerse' inn, owned by Pieter I Adornes, once stood.

9/ Philipstockstraat. It was at the start of this street that the St. Peter's Bridge crossed the Kraanrei canal. This was where Pieter I Adornes set up his exchange office, next to House 'De Matte' (no. 2).

10/ Market Square. The Water Hall was on the left, with the cage in which people could be locked up for public humiliation as a punishment.

11/ Burg Square with the town hall, where the aldermen held their meetings. The St. Donatian Church, with its chapter school, once stood directly opposite.

12/ Sint-Jansplein. It was in this square, in the Sint-Jans (St. John's) Church, that Anselm and Margareta were married. Roughly on the spot where the Hemelsdaele Lyceum now stands, Jan de la Coste, named Adornes once owned a large patrician mansion known as 'De Lecke', where he lived with his family. Adjoining this mansion, he also owned four houses on the Sint-Jansplaats and four more in the Sint-Walburgastraat.

13/ St. Walburga Church. In the 18th century, the Brotherhood of Our Lady of the Dry Tree transferred their activities to the St. Walburga Church. The 1607 triptych by Pieter Claeissens refers to this confraternity.

14/ Adornes domain. The original Adornes domain encompassed all the ground between the Rolweg, Kruisvest, Stijn Streuvelsstraat, Peperstraat and Balstraat.

15/ Guido Gezelle Museum. This piece of ground to the rear of the Adornesdomain was gifted by Pieter II to the St. Sebastian archery guild, who moved their activities to the Carmerstraat in 1573 (you can just see the little tower in the distance).

16/ Corner of the Balstraat and the Rolweg. Part of the original 15th century wall of the Adornesdomain.

17/ Balstraat 16. The Lace Centre and Lace Museum are now housed in the buildings of the 18th century lace school that was part of the Adornesdomain and is still owned by the de Limburg Stirum family.

18/ Balstraat. The west side of the Jerusalem Chapel. At the bottom of the staircase tower leading to the main chapel tower, the symbols of the Adornes family are clearly visible: in the centre, the family coat of arms and the chain of the Order of the Unicorn, with sunburst clouds alongside.

19/ Jerusalem Chapel. Note the family coat of arms in coloured brick in the front gable (just above the small window in the middle of the gable). To its right, a cross on a pedestal in vitrified brick has also been built into the same gable.

■ **Front of the Jerusalem Chapel.**

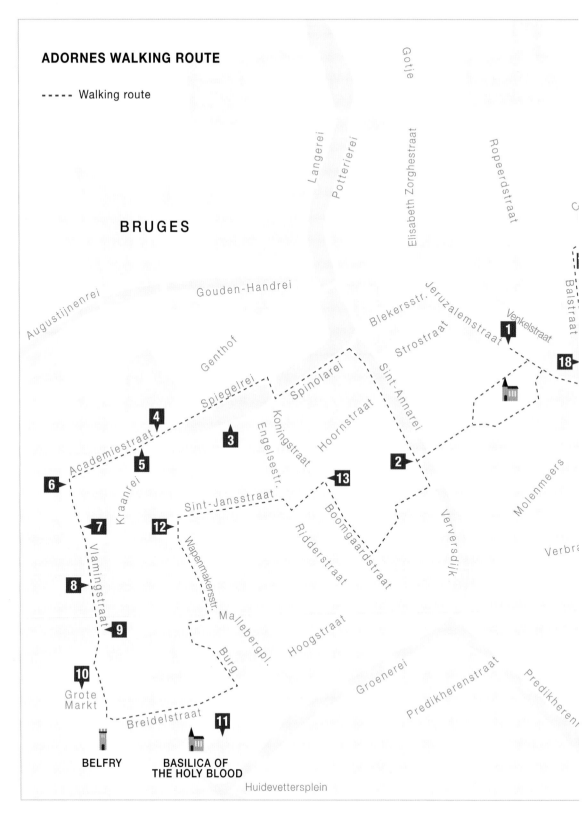

ADORNES WALKING ROUTE

----- Walking route

BRUGES

Gotje

Langerei

Potterierei

Elisabeth Zorghestraat

Ropeerdstraat

Augustijnenrei

Gouden-Handrei

Genthof

Spiegelrei

Blekerssstr.

Jeruzalemstraat

Venkelstraat

Balstraat

1

18

Strostraat

Spinolarei

Sint-Annarei

4

Academiestraat

5

Koningstraat

Engelsestr.

Hoornstraat

3

13

2

Molenmeers

6

Kraanrei

Sint-Jansstraat

Ridderstraat

Boomgaardstraat

Verversdijk

Verbra

7

12

Wapenmakersstr.

8

Vlamingstraat

9

Mallebergpl.

Hoogstraat

10

Burg

Grote
Markt

Groenerei

Predikherenstraat

Predikheren

Breidelstraat

11

BELFRY

BASILICA OF
THE HOLY BLOOD

Huidevettersplein

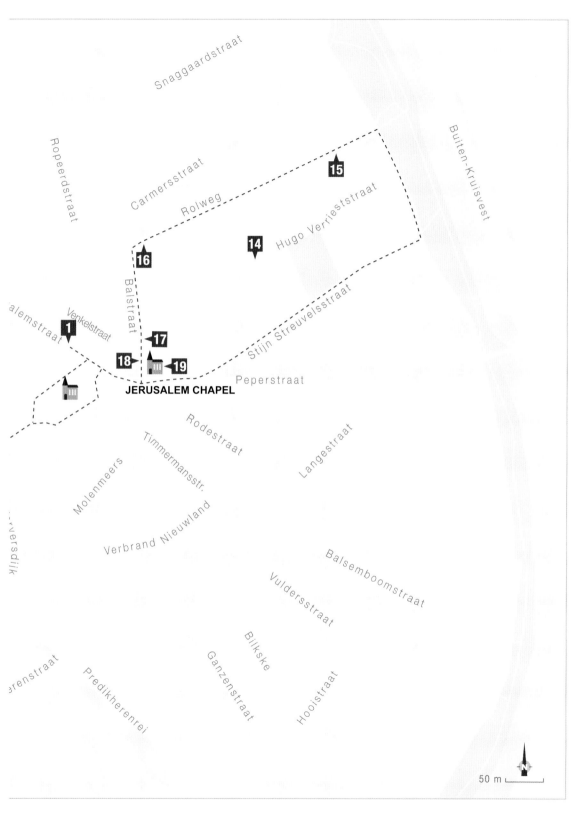

Snaggaardstraat

Ropeerdstraat

Carmersstraat

Rolweg

15

Buiten-Kruisvest

Hugo Verrieststraat

14

16

Balstraat

Stijn Streuvelsstraat

alemstraat

Venkelstraat

1

17

18

19

JERUSALEM CHAPEL

Peperstraat

Rodestraat

Langestraat

Timmermansstr.

Molenmeers

Verbrand Nieuwland

Balsemboomstraat

versdijk

Vuldersstraat

enenstraat

Predikherenrei

Ganzenstraat

Bilkske

Hooistraat

50 m

Short bibliography

C. De Maegd, 'Le Domaine Adornes à Bruges. I. La Fondation Adornes et la chapelle de Jérusalem', in: Demeures Historiques et Jardins, 195 (2017-3) 5-19.

Id., 'Le Domaine Adornes à Bruges. II. La demeure', in: Demeures Historiques et Jardins, 196 (2017-4) 5-26.

N. Geirnaert en A. Vandewalle, *Adornes en Jeruzalem. Internationaal leven in het 15ᵈᵉ- en 16ᵈᵉ-eeuwse Brugge*, Bruges, 1983.

N. Geirnaert, *Het archief van de familie Adornes en de Jeruzalemstichting te Brugge. Dl. I: Inventaris. Dl. II: Regesten van de oorkonden en brieven tot en met 1500*, Bruges, 1987 en 1989 *(Brugse geschiedbronnen uitgegeven door het Stadsbestuur van Brugge, 19 en 20)*.

Id., 'Adornes, Anselm', in: *Nationaal biografisch woordenboek*, 12 (1987) 2-13.

Id., 'Adornes, Jacob', *Ibid.* 13-15.

Id., 'Adornes, Jan', *Ibid.* 15-19.

Id., 'Adornes, Pieter I', *Ibid.* 19-21.

Id., 'Adornes, Pieter II', *Ibid.* 21-25.

J. Heers en G. De Groër (eds.), *Itinéraire d'Anselme Adorno en Terre Sainte (1470-1471)*, Paris, 1978 *(Sources d'histoire médiévale publiées par l'Institut de recherche et d'histoire des textes)*.

J. Koldeweij, 'Bruges: Jérusalem en Flandre', in: Foi et Bonne Fortune. Parure et Dévotion en Flandre Médiévale, Arnhem, 2006, 176-193.

V. Lambert en P. Stabel, *Golden Times. Wealth and Status in the Middle Ages,* Tielt, 2016.

M. Ryckaert, A. Vandewalle, J. D'Hondt, *Bruges: L'histoire d'une ville Européenne,* Tielt, 1999.

Copyrights